DISCOVERING JAPANESE
HANDPLANES

ACKNOWLEDGMENTS

To my father, Jerry, who taught me always to watch and listen; and to my daughter, Josephine, who stands on her grandfather's shoulders watching, listening, and learning—and teaching all of us.

I would also like to acknowledge the untiring support of Kathy Tam, the helpful guidance of technical editor Rick Mastelli, and the encouragement and long hours of Jerry Konicek, whose Woodworking Academy gave me the opportunity to verify and refine my techniques.

All illustrations by Scott Wynn.

Photos by Rick Mastelli, Scott Wynn, and Mike Mihalo.

© 2017 by Scott Wynn and Fox Chapel Publishing Company, Inc., 903 Square Street, Mount Joy, PA 17552.

Discovering Japanese Handplanes is an original work, first published in 2017 by Fox Chapel Publishing Company, Inc. Portions of this book appeared in *Woodworker's Guide to Handplanes* by Scott Wynn. The drawings and illustrations contained herein are copyrighted by the author. Readers may make copies for personal use. The drawings and illustrations, however, are not to be duplicated for resale or distribution under any circumstances. Any such copying is a violation of copyright law.

ISBN 978-1-56523-886-2
Library of Congress Cataloging-in-Publication Data

Names: Wynn, Scott.
Title: Discovering Japanese handplanes / Scott Wynn.
Description: East Petersburg : Fox Chapel Publishing, [2017] | Includes index.
Identifiers: LCCN 2017003864 | ISBN 9781565238862 (pbk.)
Subjects: LCSH: Woodwork. | Planes (Hand tools)--Japan.
Classification: LCC TT186 .W958 2017 | DDC 684/.082--dc23
LC record available at https://lccn.loc.gov/2017003864

To learn more about the other great books from Fox Chapel Publishing, or to find a retailer near you, call toll-free 800-457-9112 or visit us at *www.FoxChapelPublishing.com*.

Printed in Singapore
First printing

DISCOVERING JAPANESE
HANDPLANES

*Why This Traditional Tool Belongs
in Your Modern Workshop*

Scott Wynn

Author of *Getting Started with Handplanes*

FOX CHAPEL
PUBLISHING

CONTENTS

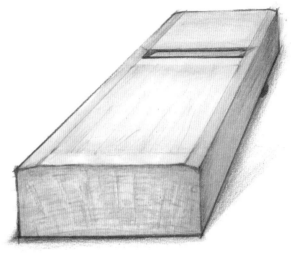

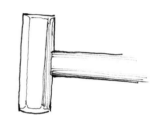

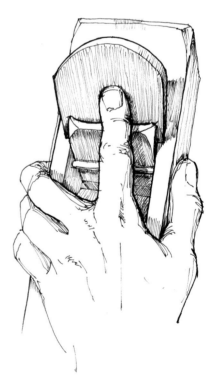

INTRODUCTION

I began woodworking in the late 1960s, a move to be expected, I suppose, because I was raised in a family of cabinetmakers, patternmakers, turners, gunsmiths, and house builders. I felt it was a logical extension of the hands-on building design work I was doing at the time. I picked up what tools I could from the local hardware store and what tips I could from my relatives and a few scattered, scarce written sources. The tools available at that time were immediately disappointing. These were not the tools that built the works of art in the museums. Certainly over the course of 3,000 or more years of woodworking, our predecessors, who did all of their work by hand, had developed effective ways to maximize their efforts to produce flawless work. The hand tools available to me at that time were not capable of flawless work by any means, and what they could do took backbreaking, hand-blistering effort.

I began to look further afield, searching the available sources. In the early 1970s, I drove across the country from my home in Ohio to Berkeley, Calif., to search out an obscure Japanese-tool dealer to look at what were then exotic tools. (The drawings of them in the *Whole Earth Catalog* looked too bizarre to be real!) Those tools were a revelation—and a validation. Japanese tools were meant to be used, used hard, and to produce rapid, excellent results. Well-made hand tools *could* be a joy to use and be highly productive! I began experimenting with any I could get my hands on, identifying strengths and weaknesses, and the work for which were best suited. Moreover, I used them daily to make my living.

Clearly, I was not alone in my frustration with the quality and availability of Western tools during the rebirth of woodworking that began in the late 1970s. At that time in the San Francisco Bay Area there were a number of highly skilled craftsmen formally trained in Japan doing work and training scores of woodworkers in Japanese carpentry and the care and use of Japanese tools. The woodworking community shared this knowledge back and forth, bolstered by demonstrations of visiting craftsmen that were promoted by Japanese manufacturers and the two importers of Japanese hand tools in the Bay Area. This tradition continues today.

There has since been a resurge in the quality of Western hand tools, planes in particular. These tools are more familiar to us and now are capable of producing better work than in previous decades. In addition, James Krenov was one of those who spearheaded the woodworking revival, and his handmade planes have a great allure. Norris-style planes were rediscovered; who could resist the beautiful combinations of steel, brass, and exotic hardwoods? But none of these planes have the *blades*. The *blades* are nearly an afterthought; they're like an excuse to build an elaborate, expensive mechanism. You can spend a week's salary on a Norris reproduction and the blade you get is cut from common flat stock; and the chipbreaker, un-hardened and not for hard use, is used more to attach the adjuster. And the elaborate mechanism is just that: elaborate, often awkward, sometimes ungainly. Or, if you're interested in productivity, you might say—slow—and expensive. Are these forms just a result of marketing? We all are attracted to the handsome pieces of machinery these tools are, but many of us use them so little we can't tell the difference in the performance of the blades, so why bother, perhaps the manufacturers are asking, to put the extra time and effort into a better blade?

If you use your planes a lot and you expect them to perform, take a look at Japanese planes.

Japanese planes are a delight to use. They are fast, efficient, effective. They sit low on the work giving great feedback and a relaxed stability. Despite the clean, lean geometric, almost modernist aesthetic of the block and blade, they accommodate the hands quite well and in a multitude of planing positions, and are quite comfortable to use for long periods. And of course the blade: individually worked to achieve a balance of resilient structure, fine grain, and a hardness that maximizes the life of the edge, the blade's cutting abilities and ease of resharpening.

Additionally, Japanese planes also can be highly effective for shaping work, because they can be easily modified or fabricated in an hour or two for same-day use. They are easy to adjust, and the adjustment is precise. Because the chipbreaker is not attached to the blade, it can be easily adjusted up or down to accommodate a variety of work, or even left off if need be. Also, partially for this reason, the blade removes quickly for re-sharpening and re-installation. Taking the blade out for sharpening requires only a few taps of a hammer; no loosening and tightening of very tight screws or tedious adjustment of the chipbreaker that tends to shift as that screw is tightened. If the blade is not particularly dull, I can knock it out, sharpen, reinstall, and adjust to use in three to four minutes. Taking the blade out, putting it back in, and adjusting it to use—without sharpening it—takes about 45 seconds. And the results from use of the plane can be stunning, as the blades available are arguably the best in the world.

Though the form is very dissimilar to Western planes, Japanese planes use the same anatomical "tactics" to do their work as do the Western planes. In this sense, they are familiar. These tactics are then altered in the same way according to the work the plane is intended to do. Unlike Western planes, however, Japanese planes are elegantly simple in concept, but complex and refined in execution. The basic plane consists of only two pieces: blade and block.

Because of the wedge-fit of the blade, and the independence of the chipbreaker, initial set-up requires instruction and perhaps some patience, but this is true of any plane from which you expect good results. Getting half-decent instruction in how to do this, does greatly speed things up (the intention of this book). I find the plane, being made of wood, does require you to pay attention to it, but otherwise, I find it to be to be surprisingly reliable and once set up, it will perform consistently with only some attention to detail. Storing the plane in a cabinet or drawer with the blade loose when not in use reduces the amount of tuning-up of the *dai* you may have to do because of temperature and humidity swings.

Some of the information I present here may break from tradition. I have been working with the planes for four decades and have made some adaptations and have experimented to better accommodate Western woods and projects, but the amount of variation from tradition is minimal, and from what I can observe, no different than you might find among individual Japanese craftsmen.

1

ANATOMY OF THE JAPANESE PLANE

The Blade

The blade is the heart of a Japanese plane; in contrast to a Western plane, often a complex and weighty construct of machined metal where the cost of the body is 10 times the cost of the blade or more, in a Japanese plane the blade may be 10 times the cost of the body, and sometimes much more. Traditionally, the blade is forge laminated and, on any plane of quality, hand-forged. This is something you will not find on a contemporary Western plane of any quality. The hand-forged blade is what sets the Japanese plane above its overelaborate competitors. Its production is the result of nearly 1,000 years of metallurgical tradition. Much of the Japanese plane's ability to cut cleanly comes from this singular ability of the blade to get incredibly sharp, and to shear without tearing. This blade, at an appropriate angle and combined with a fine throat and/or a well-set chipbreaker, will smooth the most difficult of woods.

Japanese-style smoothing planes.

Only two components constitute a complete plane: the blade and the wood block that holds it. Or four if you add a chipbreaker and its retaining pin. The plane's conceptual simplicity, however, belies its great sophistication and structural refinement. The blade itself is thick and wedge shaped and fits into a precisely cut escapement in that block of wood. (Contrary to a popular misconception, except in the

occasional specialty plane and some new, modern variations, the chipbreaker is not traditionally used to wedge the blade into position.) However, many nuances to the shape of the blade and details of the block that are not readily apparent must be attended to when setting up the plane. Besides the blade being wedge-shaped, the top face of the blade (the side opposite the bevel) is hollow ground. Much of this hollow is formed at the forge, so not much steel is removed when the blacksmith finishes it on the grinder. This hollow makes flattening the back of the blade easier, something that all blades (not just Japanese blades) must have done to them when they are first sharpened. I am always thankful the hollow is there because the steel of the laminated blade is so hard.

Figure 1-1. Japanese-Style Smooth Plane *This blade has harder pieces of steel inlaid into the top and corners to reduce mushrooming from being adjusted with a hammer; Independent chipbreaker; Tapered blade wedges into custom-fit bed and abutments; Cross pin to wedge chipbreaker*

The blade is also concave along its length on the bottom (bed side) and the plane bed must be made convex and fitted to this bevel side of the blade (and since most blades are virtually handmade, this is a custom fitting). This shaping of the blade and body is done to reduce lateral shifting of the blade during use.

The blade is also tapered across its width, being slightly narrower at the edge than at the top. This is to allow room for lateral adjustment, while still maintaining a good grip on the blade.

Figure 1-2. *The traditional Japanese blade is always laminated with hard edge steel and softer backing steel. If you look closely at the backing steel here, you can see some layering and variations that reveal its handworked origins.*

The blade angle most commonly available is about 40°, or more accurately 8 in 10 (the Japanese use a rise and run based on 10 rather than degrees. This explains some of the odd degree settings sometimes encountered.) Some suppliers will have planes with 47.5° (11 in 10). On rare occasion you might encounter 43° (9 in 10). The Japanese believe a really sharp blade is more effective than use of higher blade angles, though mainly I think it's because the vast majority of their market works softer woods. The advent of 47.5° blade angle was largely a result of one of the American suppliers requesting it from the maker for his American market. I also think the Japanese woodworker does not hesitate to make his own planes at whatever angle he thinks he needs; up until the 1930s all craftsmen made their own planes, buying the blade and the block separately.

While recently some planes have been made available with alloy and even high speed steel blades, often aimed at the less experienced or the home owner, and there have been some experiments with hi speed steel for use in difficult woods, the vast majority of blades you will encounter will be basically fine-grain carbon steel. The two most common types are what are called *white steel* and blue steel (or *white paper steel* and *blue paper steel*). They derive their name from the color of the identifying paper label applied by the steel maker (usually Hitachi). Both have carbon in the 1% to 1.4% range with .1% to .2% silica and 0.2% to 0.3% manganese. *Blue paper steels* technically are alloy steels with .2% to .5% chromium and 1% to 1.5% tungsten, with up to 2.25% tungsten in the *super blue steel*.

A PRIMER ON STEEL

The key to understanding edge steel is in its anatomy. For the needs of the woodworker, three characteristics define steel's anatomy—grain, structure, and hardness.

GRAIN

For woodworking hand tools, the grain of the steel is the most important characteristic of a blade. Ordered, repetitive arrangements of iron and alloy atoms in a crystalline structure comprise steel. The crystals can be small and fine or large and coarse. They can be consistent in size (evenly grained) or vary widely, with odd shapes and outsized clusters in among the rest. The steel's grain affects how finely the blade sharpens and how quickly it dulls. Generally, the finer and more consistent the grain, the more finely it sharpens, the slower it dulls, and the better the blade performs.

Grain is a function of the initial quality of the steel used, the alloys added, and how the steel is worked or formed. In addition to the average size of the crystals, the initial quality of the steel may include impurities, called *inclusions*, which may persist throughout refining. Inclusions add large irregularities to the grain. Irregularities sometimes are used to good effect in swords and perhaps axes, but except for the backing steel on laminated blades, impurities are a detriment to a plane blade. Sharpening impurities out to the edge causes them to break off easily, causing chipping and rapid dulling of the edge.

Alloys change the texture of the grain. They may be part of the steel's original composition (though usually in small amounts), or added in a recipe to increase the steel's resistance to shock and heat. Alloys often coarsen the grain, so there is a trade off. While the edge of an alloy blade may be more durable, especially under adverse working conditions, it may not sharpen as finely as an unalloyed blade. To shear wood cleanly, no other attribute of an edge is more important than fineness of the edge.

A PRIMER ON STEEL *(continued)*

STRUCTURE

Structure, the second most important aspect of a woodworking blade, results from changes in the original composition of the steel because of heating it and changing its shape with a hammer (or rollers), often called *hot work*. Heat causes the crystals of the steel to grow. Hammering steel when it is hot causes its crystalline structures to fracture and impedes growth as the grains fracture into smaller crystals. Before being hot-worked, the crystals of steel are randomly oriented, and frequently inconsistent in size. Through forging (repeatedly re-shaping with a hammer while the steel is hot), the grain aligns and knits together in the direction of the metal flow. Proper forging increases grain structure consistency. When exposed at the edge through sharpening, crystals consistent in size and orientation break off one at a time and dull the blade, rather than breaking off randomly in big clumps. The consistency of the crystals allows for a sharper blade that stays sharp longer.

The techniques used in preparing steel for woodworking tools are hammer forging, drop forging, and no forging. Hammer forging, where repeated hammer blows shape the steel, is the most desirable because it aligns the grain particles (or crystals) of the steel. It is a time-consuming, skillful process and therefore expensive. If improperly done, hammer forging stresses the steel, reducing, rather than increasing reliability. With the general decline in hand-woodworking skills during the last century, and the increased reliance on power tools, the discriminating market that would appreciate the difference forging makes has shrunk considerably. As a result, hand-forged tools are not commonly manufactured or available in the United States, but are still the prevalent method of producing plane blades, chisels, and other edge tools in Japan.

Drop forging verges on die cutting. A large mechanized hammer called the punch drops on the heated blank, smashing it into a die (mold), giving the tool blade its rough shape, often in just one blow. Drop forging imparts a marginally more consistent structure than a blade cut or ground from stock, because the steel often elongates in the process resulting in some improvement in the crystalline structure alignment. Drop forging is a common way of producing chisels in the West.

Drop forging is preferable to no forging at all. No forging is an over-simplification because all tool steel receives some hot work during reshaping. Bar stock is hot-formed by rolling or extruding the ingot into lengths of consistent cross section. The process rearranges the crystalline structure and the crystals tend to align in the direction of the flow as the steel lengthens. However, the arrangement is not very refined compared with the structure resulting when steel is hot-worked further at the forge. Modern Western plane blades, even many after-market premium blades, are usually ground from unworked, rolled stock.

HARDNESS

Hardness is a major selling point in the advertising of woodworking tools made from various types of steel. However, as explained earlier, grain and structure are the most important factors in the performance of a blade.

Hardness must be in balance with the intended use of the tool. High-impact hand tools, such as axes, should be softer than plane blades. Otherwise, the edge fractures quickly under the pounding an ax takes. The blades of fine tools for fine work can be very hard, but if their hardness exceeds the ability of the steel to flex without breaking at the microscopic edge, the tool will be next to worthless. It is the task of the bladesmith to produce blades that are in balance.

The *Rockwell C (Rc)* scale measures the hardness of woodworking blades. This is a unit of measurement determined by the impact of a ball-shaped point into the steel measured in terms of the depth of the resulting impression. Decent plane blades are in the range of 60–66 Rc range. Only some finely wrought steels work effectively in the upper-half of this range, principally high-quality hand-forged Japanese blades, and some high-alloy steels. In carbon steels, Rc 66 seems to be a limit above which the edge breaks down too rapidly in use, though I have heard of a Japanese master blacksmith who has made it a personal goal to develop steel that will hold an edge at about Rc 68. However, his experiments have not been available commercially.

The tungsten makes the blue steel harder to forge but increases its wear resistance when cutting difficult woods. On the other hand, adding tungsten widens the critical temperature range needed for hardening the steel, and makes this step a little easier for the blacksmith. In contrast, some white steels are fussy about their hardening temperatures. White steel is easier to sharpen, and takes the keen edge necessary for soft woods.

The difference between white and blue steel is subtle. A Japanese woodworker I know makes an enlightened distinction between the two. He describes white steel as having a sharp, angular grain structure, and blue steel as having smaller, rounded grains. This allows the white steel to be sharpened a nuance sharper, but under harsh conditions or with difficult woods white steel's grain structure breaks off a little quicker and in slightly larger clumps. For that reason, dealers often recommend blue steel for working hard, abrasive, or difficult tropical woods.

Both white and blue steel are too hard to use for the whole blade; it is too susceptible to shock and prone to cracking during use (it is also too expensive). It would also be too difficult to sharpen a blade made entirely of such hard steel. Instead, a thin layer of it is forge-welded (laminated) to a back of softer steel that has more tensile strength. The combination is better able to absorb shock without breaking.

The backing steel used for these blades is a low-carbon, softer, and more flexible steel.

Figure 1-3. Fine Japanese Blade and Chipbreaker by Blacksmith Miyamoto Masao. *If you look closely at the edge of the chipbreaker, you can see the color difference that distinguishes the edge steel from the backing steel.*

It is basically wrought iron with impurities: before the mid-nineteenth century, smelting techniques allowed the inclusion of impurities, which in the grain structure appear as strands, somewhat similar to the glass in fiberglass. The impurity increases the steel's flexibility and resistance to breaking—both desirable qualities. However, because the smelting process improved after the 1850s, steel produced since then lacks these impurities. Scrap iron produced earlier is highly coveted by Japanese blacksmiths who stockpile these treasures, such as pre-1850 anchor chain, for future use as backing steel in laminated blades.

The Chipbreaker

The best chipbreakers are also laminated, like the blades (Figure 1-4). And in all but the very cheapest planes, the chipbreaker has at least had its edge hardened and tempered; again, not a feature you will find in any Western plane. Chipbreakers do get dull, especially when they are repeatedly set close to the edge for difficult work. The Japanese chipbreakers extend the time between required maintenance; they are also easier to make sharp and crisp and to use set right down to the edge without wearing out or leaving gaps that catch the chip. The chipbreaker has two ears on the top end which are bent or straightened slightly to give the right amount of wedging action against the cross pin. The ears also provide adjustability for the wedging action of the chipbreaker, so it contacts the blade tightly and securely.

The *Dai*

The block of wood that holds the blade—it's a single block, not a laminate—is called the

Figure 1-4. How to Hold the Plane *The Japanese-style plane is normally pulled in use, though it can, of course be pushed, and the smaller planes are surprisingly comfortable when used like this. I sometimes push the plane on the jobsite when holding is awkward and I have to remove a lot of wood. Here, a Japanese-style compass plane, its sole shaped to a gentle curve, smoothes the sweep of a bench seat.*

dai. It's a very dense oak, called *kashi* either white or red, though one reliable source (only one) says it is a type of cherry; perhaps this discrepancy may be due to a confusion over scientific names. White *kashi* is generally preferred as it tends to be denser and heavier, but I have experienced pieces of red *kashi dai* that were far denser than almost any wood I've worked; my chisel almost bounced off one piece I worked with. The trees are 40 to 70 years old and are felled between late December and early March; trunk diameters are from 30cm to 50cm. Until the 1920s the blanks for the *dai* were split, giving material that last better and is resistant to warping, but now it is all sawn to size. The *dai*-maker buys his blanks from the sawmill and stores them for two to three years before fitting blades to them. Incidentally, the *dai*-maker has no part in the production of the blade or chipbreaker; that is another trade. He merely fits them individually to the block.

The whole concept of the Japanese plane with its wedge shaped blade is based on the resiliency of the wood block that holds it. The wood must not give too much as this may result in blade chatter or the blade losing its adjustment. But it must give some—just the right amount—or the blade would not be adjustable. If you're making your own planes, finding a substitute for the woods traditionally used in Japan is tricky.

The plane is meant to be pulled rather than pushed (see Figure 1-4), and the Japanese apparently are virtually the only

RELIABILITY

Japanese planes have a reputation for having to be tuned a lot. I have not found them to move any more than any other wood plane, but, because I expect a high degree of performance from my planes, I always check them before using. You can greatly reduce maintenance by proper storage.

When you are done using the plane, or at the end of the day, whichever comes first, always fully loosen the blade and then gently tap it and the chipbreaker back in just enough to keep them from falling out when you pick the plane up. Store it in a drawer or cabinet closed off to reduce temperature and humidity swings. (It is always a good idea to keep your shop at a consistent humidity as best you can year round, anyway.) Traditional houses and workshops in Japan were wide open to the air with only a hibachi for heat. Without central heating, and both summers and winters being humid, wide swings in humidity were unknown. (For that matter, the same was true in Europe until barely 30 years ago.)

woodworking culture where this is true. Many woodworking traditions have a few pulled tools, but not even their Asian neighbors, from whence their tools were derived, have major planes that are pulled. This may have evolved because the majority of Japanese craftsmen sit while they work, the cabinetmakers and furniture makers using an inclined planing board set on the floor. The board has a stop on the near end and slopes toward the user, allowing an efficient, ergonomic movement. On a wide piece, the work is shifted along the stop with the foot in between strokes of the plane. (See *The Workbench Book* by Scott Landis, Taunton Press, 1987, for more details on Japanese benches and working style.)

2

How a Plane Works

*Techniques for Achieving
Best Performance*

Though Japanese planes may look different than those from the West and other cultures, they all share a common anatomy; that is, they all work the same. Understanding these anatomical similarities is key to getting the most out of your handplane.

Figure 2-1. *All planes, including this Bailey-style iron Jack and Japanese-style Jack plane use the same anatomical tactics to produce efficient, quality work.*

THE TACTICS

These core techniques for efficient, effective performance involve six anatomical features common to all styles of handplanes, including Japanese planes:

1. **Angle of the blade to the work.** Using planes with blade angles suited to the wood or to the task increases a plane's reliability and efficiency.

2. **Clearance of the mouth through which the shaving passes.** Little understood and often abused, a suitable mouth opening controls, if not eliminates, tearout.

3. **The use of a chipbreaker.** A relatively recent invention that nearly eliminates tearout while increasing a plane's versatility.

4. **Angle of the blade's bevel.** Not having the correct blade bevel angle causes many headaches.

5. **Shape of the blade edge.** The re-sharpened edges of a plane's blade are not all straight—in fact, few of them are.

6. **Length of the plane body and width of the blade.** The two have a relationship to each other and define a plane's intended use.

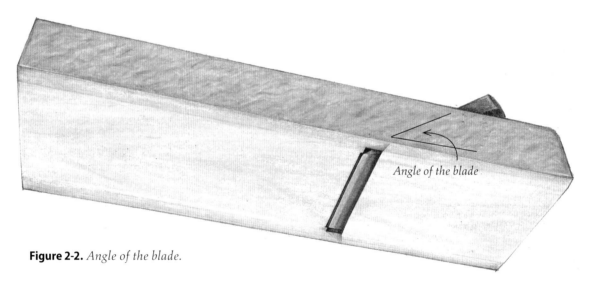

Angle of the blade

Figure 2-2. *Angle of the blade.*

1. Angle of the Blade

Most woodworkers take this aspect of the handplane for granted because it is built into the plane and the availability of new planes with different blade angles has been limited. The response of different woods to different blade angles is not necessarily pronounced, except with extremely hard and extremely soft woods. But with more demanding projects in difficult woods, matching the blade angle to the work becomes a powerful asset leading to better and more consistent results, and more efficient work.

Studying traditional tools and the woods they worked, and a fact bourn out in practice, results in the conclusion that softer woods take a lower cutting angle than the harder woods. Conversely, the harder the wood, the higher the angle. This is not always true, but it is a good starting point. I would add: Use the lowest cutting angle that remains effective, for two reasons. The lower angle shears wood fibers rather than scrapes them, producing a better surface. The lower angle also involves less work as the shearing cut presents less resistance than the scraping cut.

It is, of course, not quite that straightforward. A number of factors interplay with this rule of thumb. First, softwoods, hardwoods, and tropical hardwoods each respond differently to the cutting action of the blade.

Softwoods require cutting, not scraping. The higher cutting angles that, in hardwoods, produce successful compression failure (Type-II chips, per Bruce Hoadly in *Understanding Wood*) will only tear the fibers in softwoods, causing the chip to crumple into a bunch: a scraper will shape, but not actually smooth, softwood. The thinness and sharpness of the blade is particularly important in softwoods (Figure 2-3).

Hardwoods are on the cusp between softwoods and tropical hardwoods. Hardwoods often respond well to a sharp low-angle blade, and smoothing is possible with just a scraper. The variety of grain structures and hardness within hardwoods suggests using a variety of cutting angles. Low-to-medium blade angles work well, though higher blade angles are sometimes safer and more predictable, producing less tearout with less adjustment, maintenance, and sharpening. The resulting surface,

Figure 2-3. *This is a particularly fine example of an 8/10- (40°-) pitch Japanese-style smoothing plane with 70mm-wide, hand-forged, acid-etched blade and chipbreaker. The acid etch brings out the grain pattern of the softer backing steel. The fine blade and low cutting angle make it particularly good at finishing softwoods.*

BLADE STEELS FOR DIFFERENT WOODS

Softwoods respond best to a fine-grained steel blade sharpened to a thin, sharp edge, mounted at a low angle for a shearing cut. For this reason, a high-quality hand-forged white-steel blade is the best choice for smoothing softwood.

Although the sharpness of a fine-grained edge is not as critical, North American and European hardwoods respond best to a sharp edge. For final tearout-free smoothing, either a finely wrought white- or blue-steel blade will give you good results.

Tropical hardwoods are less sensitive to the thinness of the cutting edge. Tropical hardwoods do not demand the sharpness required by the softwoods and most hardwoods for good results. They cut best with a high-angle blade—more of a scraping cut. The wood's hardness generates a fair amount of heat at the blade's edge. Under such conditions, and considering the abrasive nature of some of these woods, a thin edge is more susceptible to rapid dulling, minor chipping, or other damage. Using a blue steel or super blue steel or even a good fine-grained alloy steel blade makes sense here.

Figure 2-4. *In this set of traditional Western-style planes for use on hardwoods, the higher the pitch, the smoother the surface produced. From front to back: try plane with a 43° pitch; jointer with a 47½° pitch; smoother with a 50° pitch.*

Figure 2-5. *A set of Chinese cabinet-makers planes for use on tropical hardwoods, back to front: jointer with a 55° pitch; intermediate smoother with a 60° pitch; smoother with a 65° pitch. The size of the intermediate smoother varies from woodworker to woodworker. Sometimes it is about the same size as the jointer but with a higher pitch and finer set-up; sometimes it is about the size of a Western jack plane, as shown here.*

BLADE ANGLES FOR DIFFERENT WOODS

As a general rule of thumb, the plane-blade angle for softwoods varies from 35° to around 45° with the lower end working best. Blade angles for hardwoods run the gamut from about 40° to 55° and higher, though the majority works well in the 45° to 50° range. Tropical hardwood blade angles ranges from about 50° to over 65°.

though, is not as smooth or clear as with a lower-angle cut (Figure 2-4).

Tropical hardwoods respond well to scraping, conversely tearing out disastrously at low and intermediate blade angles. Traditional blade angles for tropicals often are quite high—at what would be a scraping angle in a softer wood. Despite the high angle, the plane blade leaves a clean-cut surface with good clarity (Figure 2-5).

There is a great deal of overlap where angles work well in a particular wood (Figure 2-6). Often the same angle seems less effective from one board to another in the same species, or even from one part of a board to another. Because of such variations, most woodworkers use more conservative angles— slightly steeper but within the acceptable range—for more predictable results and little or no tearout. In practice, I begin preparing a piece with a 40° Japanese plane to see how the board responds and step up to a steeper-angle plane if the wood requires it. In some instances the Japanese may prepare a surface with higher angle blades since they tend to be a bit more reliable, and then, depending on the finish to be applied, may finish with a finally set lower angle blade to finely shear and polish the surface.

Finally, you will find some blade angles cannot be used when cutting some woods. It is not that they do not cut well, but that they nearly do not cut at all. Pine, for instance, seems to crumple as the blade angle increases over 45°. Results can be disastrous with some tropical hardwoods at even the intermediate blade angles.

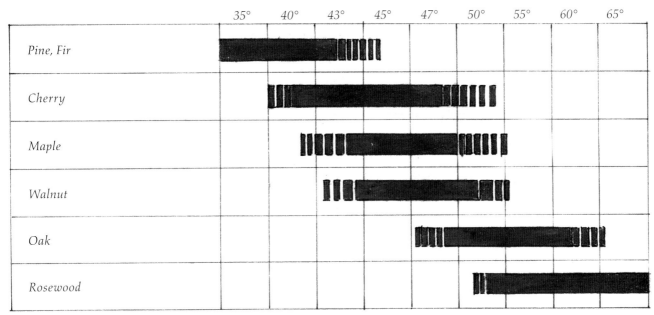

Figure 2-6. *Within the range for each wood, the lower angles are generally for preparatory planes. The higher angles are for smoothing planes.*

BLADE ANGLE AND THE TASK

Studying traditional tools also shows the cutting angle of a plane blade depends upon the task being performed (you can see this in Figures 2-4 and 2-5). Because a lower-angle blade presents less resistance in cutting than a higher-angle blade with its scraping cut, planes used for shaping or preparing stock tend to have lower angles. Lower-cutting angles are less fatiguing because the plane requires less effort to push. At this stage in the work, stock removal is more important than smoothness, which can be accomplished with succeeding planes. Traditionally, craftsmen working in hardwood use several planes to take a board from initial surfacing to final smoothing. Each succeeding plane had a slightly steeper pitch, usually finishing with a plane the craftsman determines has the optimal angle for the work produced.

Softwoods are the exception to this: There is no marked improvement in either ease or

THE JAPANESE BLADE

The Japanese believe a low shearing cut with an extremely sharp blade is the best approach to a smooth cut. They depend heavily on the quality of their blades, their ability to get them sharp, and their technique in planing. The plane I use most is a 40° 70mm (2 ¾") Japanese plane that works well on woods most Westerners would not touch with a plane having such a low blade angle. The blade's quality and resharpenability are the reasons it is such a capable tool.

PITCH ANGLES

While Western blade angles are usually measured in degrees, the pitch of a Japanese plane blade is determined using a rise/run scale based on 10 rather than degrees. That is why you will sometimes come across such apparently odd pitches as 47½°, which is actually a rise of 11 in a run of 10. Curiously, some of these pitches can be found also in English planes. Norris planes often had a pitch of 47½°, and I have an American razee try plane with a 43° blade angle (a 9 in 10 pitch). As it turns out, these are my favorite blade angles for smoothing wood; 43° degrees does a nice job on many of the softer hardwoods, as well as maple, and 47½° works well on many of the harder hardwoods. The latter pitch also seems to be a critical angle around which the geometry of the cut begins to change.

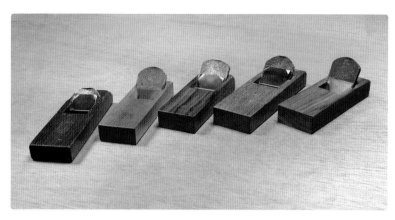

Figure 2-7. *Make planes as you need them, like one of these 48mm Japanese planes with different blade angles. The plane at front, over 30 years old, has a 40° pitch and I regularly use it on the jobsite. Behind that is my first shopmade plane, about 25 years old, with a 43° pitch and no chipbreaker. The remaining three are a 43°-pitch plane with a chipbreaker, shopmade with a canary wood dai; a commercial plane with a 47 ½° pitch and a red oak dai; and a 55° shopmade plane, single-bladed with a canary wood dai.*

Figure 2-8. *Here are three custom planes, left to right: 70mm blade at 43° pitch; 70mm blade at 47 ½° pitch; 55mm blade at 53° pitch.*

Figure 2-9. *These chibi-kannas, or finger planes, were very effective in fairing out the long sweeping curves of this carving.*

quality of cut by increasing the blade angle. Softwoods cut best at 35° to 40°; they do need an exceedingly sharp blade and a thin bevel, however, to give their best results.

CUSTOM BLADE ANGLES

If you utilize wood you suspect would work more easily or predictably with a blade angle different from what is commonly available, you should make your own (Figure 2-7). A woodworker of intermediate skill can readily make a Japanese plane. With a little extra time, a novice can make one as well. The trick is to know the simple technique. With some practice, a single-blade Japanese plane with a 45mm (1 ¾") blade (no chipbreaker) takes around one and one-half to two hours (the first one will take longer). Moreover, it is usable the same day, because you do not have to wait for the glue to dry. (See "Making a Japanese-Style Plane" on page 122.)

Once you have the confidence to make a plane, you can experiment making specialty planes to solve specific problems (Figure 2-8). I have made simple molding planes to match antique work where I needed only a few feet of molding. In addition, I have made planes to assist in effects on carved work (Figure 2-9).

2. Mouth Opening

Controlling the shaving as it passes through the opening in the bottom of the plane is probably the second-most basic technique for controlling tearout, but one that is not well understood (Figure 2-11). Restricting the throat opening (Figure 2-12) works to reduce tearout by compressing the wood

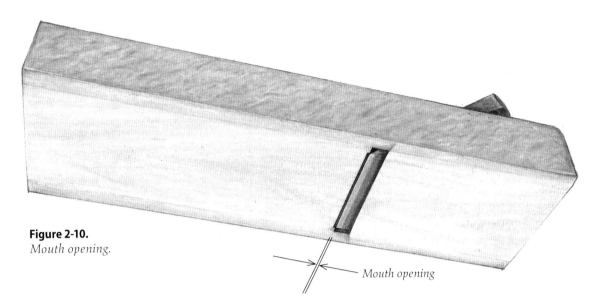

Figure 2-10.
Mouth opening.

Mouth opening

fibers immediately in front of the blade, thus keeping them from splitting out ahead of the cut (Figure 2-13). While it is an effective tactic, it has become a less popular one for a number of reasons.

For one, the amount of openness is a dynamic factor, affected by the combination of blade angle, chipbreaker bevel angle, and escape angle of the throat

The result of such complexity is easy to misjudge, and can be frustrating. If the mouth is too small for the cut, the shavings jam in the throat, which can damage the edge of the mouth and sometimes the blade. Restricting the chip at the mouth of the plane definitely increases stress on the blade, as both pressure and heat build. The increased downward pressure on the blade due to the chip being constricted as it passes through the mouth—made even greater at the higher blade angles—increases the importance of the correct bevel angle, as the blade edge is liable to flex. (See "Bevel Angle" on page 27.) When this happens, it flexes deeper into the cut, taking a slightly thicker chip. The result is one of three things: tearout, a chattering cut (as the blade flexes back and

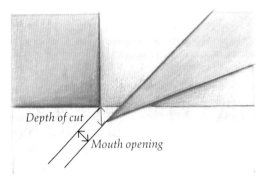

Depth of cut

Mouth opening

Figure 2-11.
For maximum effectiveness against tearout, the mouth opening is equal to the depth of cut. In the real world, the mouth may have to be ever so slightly larger, but definitely no less than the depth of cut.

Figure 2-12. *Shaving restrained by a tight mouth opening prevents shaving from lifting ahead of the cut, reducing or eliminating tearout.*

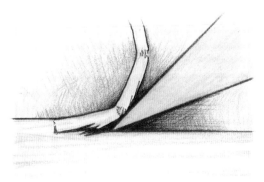

Figure 2-13. *Unrestrained shaving splits out ahead of cut, causing tearout.*

forth), or a chip too large for the opening, which causes the chip to jam (Figure 2-14).

Closing the mouth down also increases the wear on the edge of the mouth itself. For maximum effectiveness, the edge of the mouth should be crisp. Sharp is even better. The increased pressure from constricting the chip rounds the edge over pretty fast, and the rounder it gets, the less effective it is. Truing the sole repeatedly to keep this edge sharp, as well as maintain the bottom, opens the throat up over time as the blade and throat angles diverge. To solve this problem, a piece of hardwood is dovetailed into the throat of

the plane, effectively closing up the mouth. This repair is effective and renewable because it is the harder end grain bearing on the work (see Figure 2-15). In fact, new Japanese planes and plane blocks can be bought with this feature already installed. This dovetailed piece is often called a *kuchi-ire* in catalogs.

The interrelationship of the mouth opening to the other anatomical tactics is dynamic. The effectiveness of restricting the mouth opening varies according to the blade angle. While effective at lower angles, it seems more so at higher blade angles (50°-plus) and practice confirms it. The chipbreaker, however, seems to be less effective on higher-angle planes and increasingly effective as blade angle drops below 50°. On planes with angles greater than 50°, I rely on a small mouth opening alone to control tearout.

Finish planing is the only task you can do with a plane so configured because the mouth is too narrow for other work. You will need more planes because a single tool will not do a variety of tasks as designed. I believe you will find the set-up and maintenance of a fine finish plane does not lend itself to the plane doing less-refined tasks, mouth opening or not, intended versatility or not. Fine-finish planing is demanding and having dedicated planes set up for it is a timesaver.

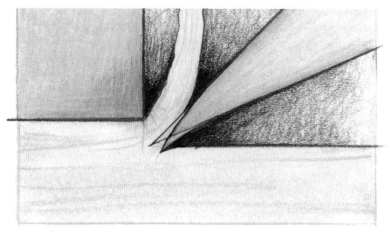

Figure 2-14. *A mouth opening or a bevel angle that is too small can cause the edge to flex.*

3. Chipbreaker

The chipbreaker is a 300- to 400-year-old invention that only reached Japan in the late 1800's. It greatly increases the reliability of the handplane in getting consistently smooth results. The chipbreaker accomplishes this through

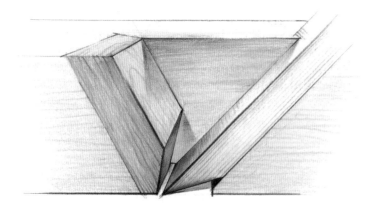

Figure 2-15. *A kuchi-ire installed as a repair to close the mouth on a wooden plane. Because end grain bears on the work, this is a durable (and re-adjustable) repair.*

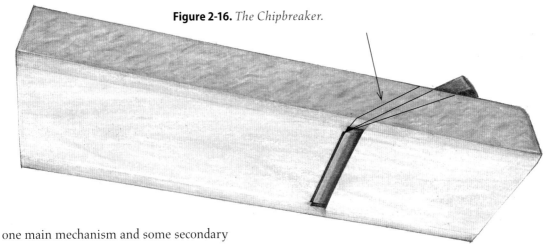

Figure 2-16. *The Chipbreaker.*

one main mechanism and some secondary ones. The primary mechanism for improving consistency of the cut gives the piece its name; by sharpening the bevel on the chipbreaker and placing it directly behind the cutting edge (Figure 2-17), the chip is broken backward before it has a chance to lift and split ahead of the cut (Figure 2-18). This has proven to be a highly effective method of reducing tearout, especially when coupled with a small mouth opening at lower-to-medium blade angles.

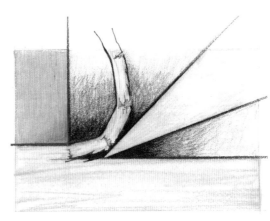

Figure 2-17. *As the shaving rides up the blade, it can lift and split out ahead of the cut.*

The Japanese chipbreaker, in contrast with the Stanley chipbreaker, for instance, is a very effective design. A very small bevel, often only ¼" (.4mm) wide, functions as the edge that breaks the chip. Behind that is a long low bevel which gives excellent clearance for the shaving (Figure 2-19). The top end of the chipbreaker has a bent tab on either side. These are alternately bent more or flattened to finesse the fit of the chipbreaker—to give it just enough

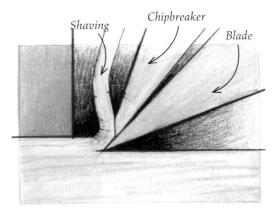

Shaving   *Chipbreaker*   *Blade*

Figure 2-18. *The chipbreaker breaks the shaving (chip) before it can ride up the blade and split out ahead of the cut.*

JAPANESE CHIPBREAKERS

Good quality Japanese planes have chipbreakers and main blades laminated with a hard steel edge. Sometimes on the lesser-quality Japanese planes, the chipbreaker is hardened tempered, not laminated. You might think this is excessive, but it is not. Using a chipbreaker in a position tight to the cutting edge, subjects it to a lot of impact and heat. It will dull and needs to be resharpened over time, and if it is not, it may begin to trap chips. I have seen soft chipbreakers get a multitude of tiny dents from just the impact of the shaving. I also have seen the discoloration on the edge from when the oils in the wood vaporize from the heat of the cut. Having a hard chipbreaker reduces maintenance and improves reliability.

pressure so that it doesn't move under working conditions. The underside is always well formed; because it is most often laminated, the underside is hollowground like the top of the blade. This means that the chipbreaker mates to the blade with a knife edge, guaranteeing a gapless fit. And because it is steel as hard as the edge, won't form a burr from pressure and movement to the blade that will catch shavings.

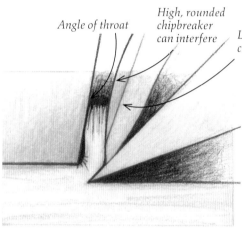

Angle of throat

High, rounded chipbreaker can interfere

Line of flat-bevel chipbreaker

Figure 2-19. *To allow the shaving to pass unobstructed, the throat of the plane should be wider at all points than the thickness of the shaving. On some Western planes, the high, rounded type of chipbreaker will obstruct the throat.*

THE CORRECT BEVEL ANGLE

There are limits and ranges you can use as rules of thumb in correcting the bevel angle. First, the minimum clearance angle on a bevel-down blade should be about 12°, although 15° would be better. This parameter will limit the size of the bevel angle on low-angle planes. For instance, if you have a plane with a 35°-cutting angle, the bevel angle of the blade is going to be limited to a maximum of 23° (35°-12°=23°). The practical lower limit of the bevel for most blades is about 22°—any smaller and the blade usually crumples at the edge in common use. Also, the bevel angle varies according to the bedding angle of the blade; the steeper the bedding angle, the greater the bevel angle should be. For instance, a plane with bedding angle of 40° could have a bevel angle of 22°; depending on the quality of the blade, 25° to 28° would probably be more serviceable; a 45° plane would have a bevel angle of 25° to 30°. A plane with a bedding angle of 55° could have a bevel angle of 30° to 32°, to perhaps as much as 35°. A bedding angle of 65° could have a bevel angle of as much as 38° to 40°.

Some woodworkers say the chipbreaker can correct chattering by *pre-tensioning* the cutting edge. However, I would not rely on the chipbreaker to correct for a too-small bevel. It is far better to give the edge its proper bevel angle. (See "Bevel Angle" on page 27.)

SETTING THE CHIPBREAKER

I think the main advantage of the chipbreaker is to increase a plane's versatility. Setting the chipbreaker down close to the edge reduces tearout and allows a more finished cut. Setting the chipbreaker back allows the blade to be more deeply set to hog off wood. All of this can happen regardless of the throat opening, which is built-in. The adjustment is accomplished most easily with a Japanese-style blade, and I have often repeatedly adjusted the chipbreaker back and forth on the Japanese plane I take to the job site to perform these two tasks. The adjustable throat of the small metal block plane provides similar versatility, one of the reasons why it is so popular with carpenters. Backing off the chipbreaker on most Western planes requires disassembly, and a screwdriver.

How close should the chipbreaker be set to the edge? Generally, the chipbreaker is set back from the edge in a distance equal to the maximum thickness of the shaving you expect to make with that plane. This is also usually equal to the amount of curve honed into the edge of the blade. (See "Shape of the Blade Edge" on page 32.) You do not want the chipbreaker set below the corners of the blade. For the finest finish work, I set the chipbreaker down until there is only the barest glint of light left on the top (back) of the blade. This is much

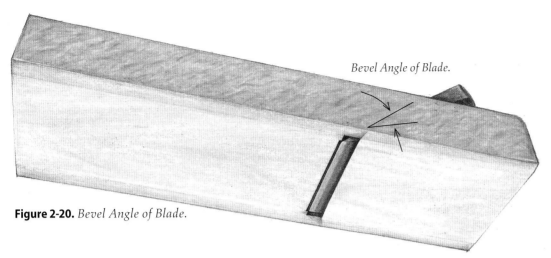

Figure 2-20. *Bevel Angle of Blade.*

less than ¼4" (.4mm) because that fine line of light tells me there is still some blade exposed. For the adjustment to work, the chipbreaker must be very well prepared (see "Prepare the Chipbreaker" on page 70) or the chips will jam.

For coarse work, the chipbreaker can be set well back, though it is usually not necessary to set it back much more than ¼6" (2mm). On planes used to prepare stock, such as the jack, the chipbreaker is usually set back a little more than the arc of the blade edge.

4. Bevel Angle

The bevel angle is the angle to which the blade is sharpened. Most blades leave the factory with a 25° or 30° bevel angle—though Japanese blades often come with a 22° bevel. To bring a plane to its finest performance, the bevel angle may well

need further attention (Figure 2-21).

If the bevel angle is too small, the edge flexes under the load, bending down until the chip releases, and then springing up to its original position (Figure 2-14 on page 24). It may do

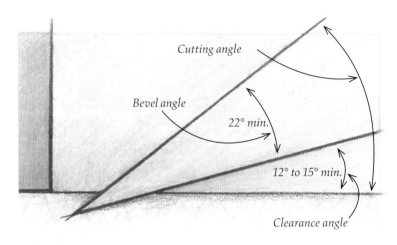

Figure 2-21. *Practical Minimum Bevel Angle and Clearance Angle.*

HOW AN EDGE DULLS

To understand why you would want the bevel angle as small as possible, study how an edge dulls. The gradual effect is that the edge rounds over. If the bevel angle is too large, the worn edge retreats from the work and the main bevel begins rubbing, which prevents the edge from contacting the work. This is exacerbated by the natural tendency of the wood to spring back slightly after the cut. The larger the bevel (on a bevel-down blade), the less the clearance angle to the work, and the sooner this action happens.

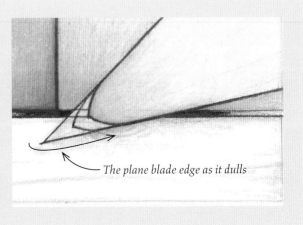

The plane blade edge as it dulls

HONING A HOLLOW-GROUND BEVEL

An argument against hollow grinding is that it thins the metal immediately behind the edge and produces a bevel angle that is too small. This happens because even though the edge is honed at the proper angle, the steel right behind that honed edge that should support it has been removed—hollowed out to the curve of the grinding wheel. If you were to draw a tangent to the curve of the grind in the area immediately behind the honed edge, you would see this is a much smaller angle than the honing angle, and could allow the blade to flex.

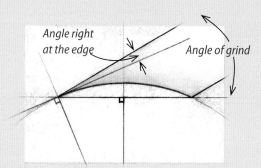

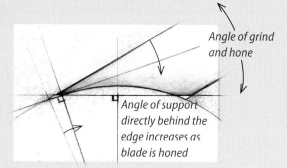

Figure 1. *The angle near the edge on a hollow-ground blade (shown here exaggerated for clarity) is much less than the overall angle to which the blade has been ground. On a ⅜"-thick blade, such as a Japanese blade, ground to 30° on a 6"-diameter wheel, the angle is roughly 7° less at the edge than the grind angle.*

Figure 2. *As the blade is honed, the hollow decreases with each sharpening, and the angle directly behind the honed edge increases. Eventually, when the bevel has been honed flat, it equals the grind angle.*

this repeatedly, resulting in chatter. Or, the blade may flex under the stress of cutting the shaving, especially if it hits a harder part of the board, diving down into the wood and cutting a chip thicker than it was set for. If the plane has a very fine mouth, instead of springing back up, the thicker chip may jam the mouth. Therefore, even though the plane is otherwise finely tuned, the mouth can continue to jam with chips.

As a rule of thumb, the bevel angle should be as small as will cut without chattering. Larger angles and a restricted mouth opening will place increased stress on the blade edge, causing it to deflect in use. Increasing the

bevel angle will alleviate this. The objective is to increase the bevel angle only enough as is required to eliminate chattering. Any more increases resistance and may reduce the smoothness of the cut. Begin with the factory angle and see how it performs. If you suspect it is too small and diagnostic checks as described in the "Troubleshooting" on page 93 indicate that is the problem, then increase the bevel angle until achieving the desired performance. Generally the 22° angle found on most Japanese blades will not be thick enough for hard work at the higher angles required for hardwoods, especially with a restricted mouth.

FOX CHAPEL
PUBLISHING

FOX CHAPEL PUBLISHING
903 SQUARE ST
MOUNT JOY PA 17552–1911

FREE Pattern OFFER!

GET Creative with these Fantastic Patterns!

YES! Please send me the Free Pattern indicated below

☐ Woodcarving ☐ Scroll Saw ☐ Pyrography ☐ Woodworking ☐ Woodturning

Name

Address   City

State/Prov.   Zip

Country

BONUS Enter your email address to receive more free patterns and special offers!

Email

Return card or complete online for instant access to free patterns:
www.foxchapelpublishing.com/free-pattern

PLANE GEOMETRY: A SUMMARY

The interrelationship between blade angle, mouth opening, chipbreaker, throat angle, and bevel angle is dynamic **(Figure 1).** When constructing or tuning a plane, keep the interplay in mind and adjust each element according to the other. *Single-bladed planes* of course, do not have a chipbreaker. Planes with a chipbreaker sometimes are called *double-iron planes*.

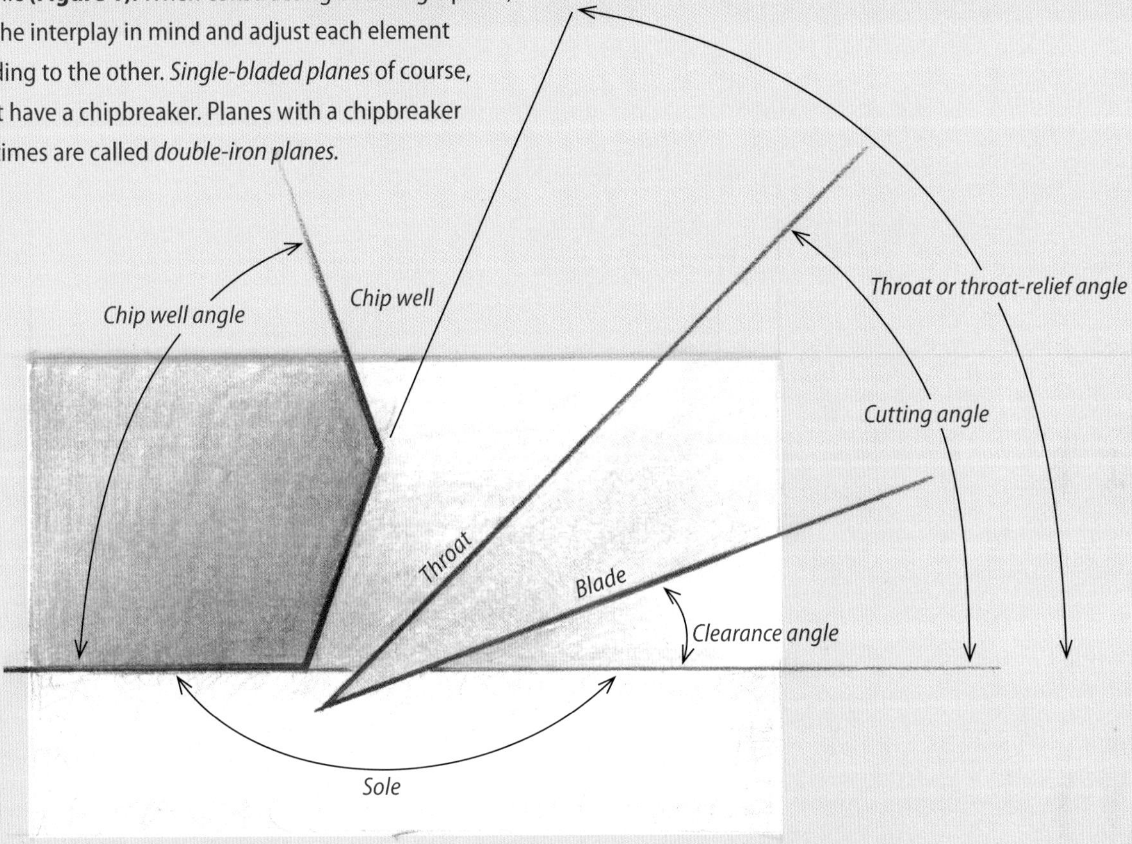

Chip well angle

Chip well

Throat or throat-relief angle

Cutting angle

Throat

Blade

Clearance angle

Sole

Figure 1. *Definitions*

SINGLE-BLADED PLANES

On planes without a chipbreaker, the mouth opening should be the same size or perhaps slightly larger than the thickest shaving you intend to make with that plane. On roughing out and dimensioning planes, the opening could be ⅟₃₂" to ⅟₁₆" (0.8mm to 2mm) or greater **(Figure 2).** On intermediate smoothing planes, a mouth opening of 0.01"

(0.25mm) or less is expected **(Figure 3).** On your finest finish planes, the mouth opening could be just several thousandths of an inch **(Figure 4).**

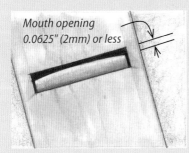

Mouth opening 0.0625" (2mm) or less

Figure 2. *Jack Plane*

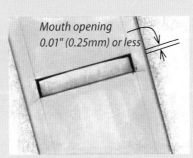

Mouth opening 0.01" (0.25mm) or less

Figure 3. *Intermediate Smoother*

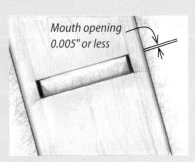

Mouth opening 0.005" or less

Figure 4. *Finish Smoother*

PLANE GEOMETRY: A SUMMARY *(continued)*

The angle of the throat opening need be only 15° to 20° greater than the cutting angle, but usually not less than 70° **(Figure 5).**

You want to keep the throat angle as small as possible because as the plane wears and the bottom is trued repeatedly, the mouth opens **(Figure 6).** Keeping the angle as small as possible slows this process and delays mouth repair.

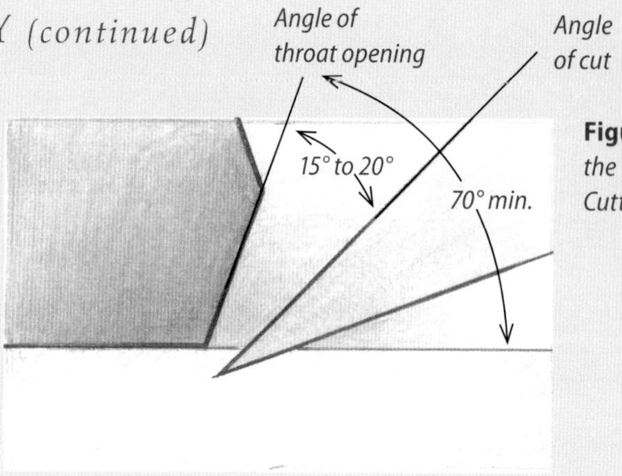

Angle of throat opening

Angle of cut

15° to 20°

70° min.

Figure 5. *Relationship of the Throat Angle to the Cutting Angle*

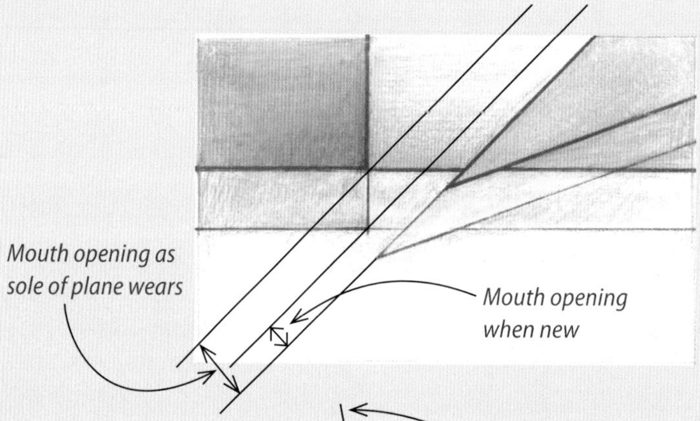

Figure 6. *As the sole of the plane wears and is flattened repeatedly, the mouth opening gradually increases in size.*

Mouth opening as sole of plane wears

Mouth opening when new

DOUBLE-IRON PLANES

Sharpen the working edge on a chipbreaker so it is 90° to 100° to the sole when mounted in the plane. Use the higher angle on low-blade-angle planes, the lower angle on high-blade-angle planes **(Figure 7).**

For maximum reduction of tearout, the chipbreaker should be set back from the edge a distance equal to about the thickness of the shaving to be cut. Depending on the curvature, the set back often equals the sweep of the blade. Of course, the chipbreaker should not be set below the bottom of the plane **(Figure 8).**

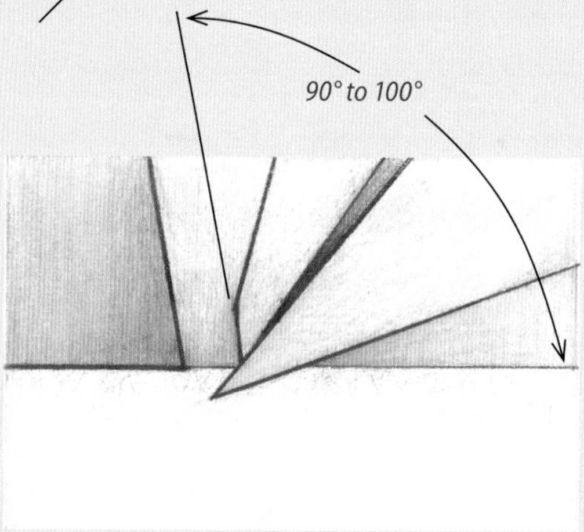

90° to 100°

Figure 7. *Angle of the Working Bevel of the Chipbreaker*

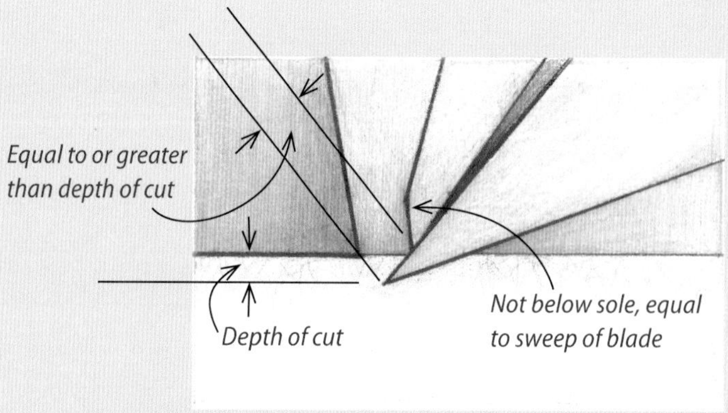

Figure 8. *Chipbreaker Setback*

Equal to or greater than depth of cut

Depth of cut

Not below sole, equal to sweep of blade

At all points, the opening for the shaving to pass must be greater than the thickness of the shaving itself. If you are trying to maximize the effect of a small mouth opening in combination with the use of a chipbreaker, the throat angle would have to be equal to, or preferably greater than, the combined angle of the blade and chipbreaker bevel, or between 90° and 100°—maybe slightly more **(Figure 9)**.

Any more, however, and the edge of the mouth can become too thin, wearing extremely quickly and sometimes even flexing under the pressure of the constrained shaving, causing the shaving to jam the throat. As the bottom of the plane flattens, the mouth also wears open quickly.

A plane set up with the smallest mouth opening and tightest chipbreaker setting can make only the finest, thinnest of cuts. For smoothing planes requiring more versatility, especially in the low-to-intermediate blade angles, it is more practical to rely mostly on the chipbreaker to eliminate tearout, with the mouth opening in a supporting role **(Figure 10)**. Such a strategy allows a reduced throat angle that will slow the gradual enlargement of the mouth opening as the sole is conditioned. In this case, the mouth opening would be no more than ¹⁄₆₄" (.4mm). Clearance for the shaving through the throat must be maintained, however.

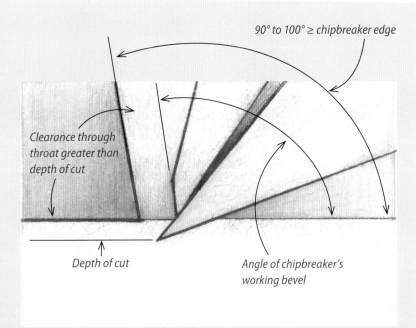

90° to 100° ≥ chipbreaker edge

Clearance through throat greater than depth of cut

Depth of cut

Angle of chipbreaker's working bevel

Figure 9. *The angle of the chipbreaker's working bevel.*

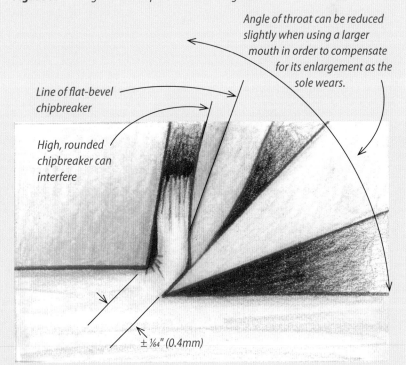

Angle of throat can be reduced slightly when using a larger mouth in order to compensate for its enlargement as the sole wears.

Line of flat-bevel chipbreaker

High, rounded chipbreaker can interfere

± ¹⁄₆₄" (0.4mm)

Figure 10. *To increase a plane's versatility, especially in planes with a blade angle of 47½° or less, it's more practical to rely on the chipbreaker than the mouth opening to reduce tearout. On a smoothing plane, however, you'll still want a mouth opening of about ¹⁄₆₄" (0.4mm).*

5. Shape of the Blade Edge

Shaping the blade edge is a traditional technique also not well understood today, but one that greatly increases the effectiveness of the handplane. The basic concept is roughing and shaping planes have blades of significant curvature across their width, smoothing and finishing planes have blades with decreasing curvature, and the final plane has a nearly straight edge. In theory, on all three planes, the curvature equals to the maximum thickness of the planned shaving. The strategy is effective for a number of reasons. On all planes, it keeps the corners of the blade from digging in and tearing up the wood at the borders of the cut. On roughing-out planes often used diagonally to the grain, it reduces tearout, the amount of effort required to push (or pull) the plane, and chip

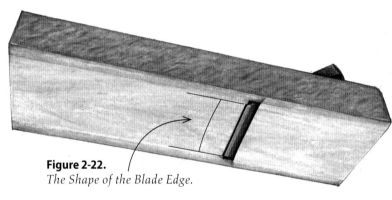

Figure 2-22.
The Shape of the Blade Edge.

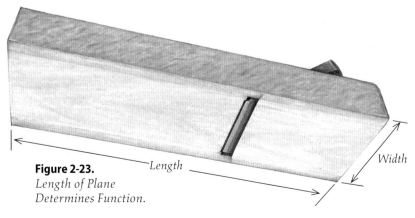

Figure 2-23.
*Length of Plane
Determines Function.*

jamming at the most likely spot—the corners of the blade. On finish planes, it eliminates steps or ridges between each cut, producing a smoother surface. On jointer planes, the slight curvature can speed up jointing edges (when not using a shooting board) and strengthen the resulting edge joint.

In all cases, the amount of curvature to the blade is equal to the maximum depth of cut you expect to make with that plane.

A few planes should have a straight edge, most notably rabbet planes. In addition, any plane used on a shooting board should have a blade with a straight edge.

6. Length of the Plane/ Width of the Blade

The length of a plane determines its intended function:

- **Long planes** true (straightening) surfaces. Their long length bridges low spots with the blade cutting the high spots down and lowering all surface points to the same plane (Figure 2-24).

- **Intermediate-length planes** handle initial stock preparation, shaping and dimensioning. A longer plane for truing often follows. Occasionally, as per the craftsman's preference, they may be set up as an intermediate plane following the longer truing plane and used to prepare the surface for final smoothing. Appropriate setup and blade shape accompanies either use (see Chapter 6, Figure 6-17, on page 74).

- **The shortest planes** are for final smoothing. They are short for the opposite reason truing planes are long—to follow the low spots. Because of the fine tolerance of their setup and use, variations in the surface of only a few ten-thousandths of an inch may cause the plane to skip over the low spots. On difficult woods, setting the blade deeper to cut to these low spots is not an option because a deeper setting may cause tearout. Shortening the plane's length helps reduce this bridging.

A corollary to the length of the plane is the configuration of the bottom of the plane. Western tradition has the bottom of all planes dead flat. However, what is flat? Is within .01" (.25mm) good enough? 0.001" (.025mm)? .0001" (.0025mm)? In addition, on what areas on the bottom of the plane would the variation be allowed?

The plane must be as flat as the finest shaving you expect to make with it (see Figure 2-25). If you intend the plane to produce shavings only 9 microns thick, as sometimes happens in Japanese planing competitions, then the bottom of the plane must be within 9 microns of flat; otherwise, the blade may be held off the work by the bottom and will not cut. If you are making a cut ¹⁄₁₆" (2mm) thick with a jack plane, then the bottom needs to be less than ¹⁄₁₆" (2mm) out of flat (although it will work better if it is flatter than that). If you are heading for very fine work, this can be a daunting proposition conceptually; practically, it is downright frightening. To flatten 16 square inches to within 9 microns, and keep it there, despite wear and variations due to heat and humidity is meticulous, nearly perpetual work.

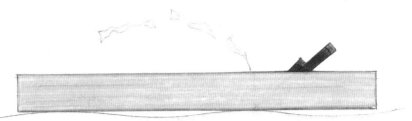

Figure 2-24. *Longer planes bridge the low spots, cut the high spots, giving a truer surface.*

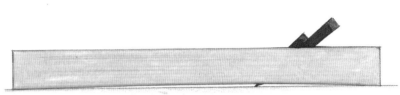

Figure 2-25. *Even though you can see the blade is adjusted to a cutting depth, it may be held off the work and prevented from cutting by the amount the sole is out of true.*

Contact areas behind the blade vary in location and number depending on the intended use of the plane.

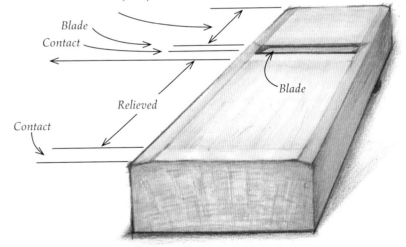

Blade
Contact
Relieved
Contact
Blade

Figure 2-26. *The sole of a Japanese plane is traditionally relieved in strategic areas to simplify maintenance.*

In response, the Japanese have a practical answer to flattening the bottom of a plane, one I use on all of my planes. The concept is only two (or three or four, depending on the type of plane or its intended use) areas need to be in a flat plane, about the width of the blade extending across the sole, and about ¼" (6mm) long. All other areas are relieved so they do not contact the work or need constant attention (Figure 2-26). This simplifies *flattening* and maintaining the sole of the plane The contact areas are then configured for the use intended for that particular plane: dimensioning, truing, or smoothing, as the shape of the wood will mirror the way the bottom of the plane is shaped.

To facilitate rapid stock removal, the contact areas of dimensioning planes are relieved in the area following the blade perhaps .01" to .02" (.25mm to .05mm). Truing planes will have all contact areas along the length of the plane in a line, to ensure stock being planed comes out straight.

Smoothing planes will have the contact area behind the blade slightly relieved—usually less than the desired thickness of the shaving (approximately .005", or .125mm)—both to help maintain flatness and to enable a very finely set blade to contact the work.

The width of the blade (and the plane) also varies according to the intended use of the plane. The blade of the truing plane (the longest plane) also tends to be the widest, about 2⅜" to 2¾" (60mm to 70mm) wide. This helps produce the flattest surface. Planes for stock preparation, such as the jack, have the narrowest blades, from about 1¾" to 2½" (48mm to 65mm). Because they are used to remove large amounts of wood, a wide cut would be too much work. Smoothing planes tend to be wider than the stock-removal planes, but just how wide is pretty much up to the crafter. The wider the blade, the less pronounced the faint scallops, which are a result of the faint curvature of the blade edge. However, a wider blade involves more setup, maintenance, and work to use. Smoothing planes, especially for hardwood, are in the range of 2" to 2⅜" (50mm to 60mm) wide, though 2¾" to 3" (70mm to 75mm) is not unheard of. Actually, I have seen Japanese planes with 6" or 8" (150mm or 200mm)-wide blades used on cedar. While they are unusual, reserved mainly for temple work, they are beautiful and make a stunning shaving and finished surface.

THE PROPORTION OF LENGTH TO WIDTH

In full-size planes, a truing plane ranges from about 18" to 30" (457mm to 762mm). Both preparation and intermediate smoothing planes range in length from about 13" to 18" (330mm to 457mm). Smoothing planes range in length anywhere from 6" to 12" (152mm to 305mm). However, it is up to the crafter to decide the best use for planes of particular lengths. The decision may have more to do with blade shape and bottom configuration than length. A plane disproportionately short for its width of blade can be useful for difficult wood. It allows a fine setting of the blade while reaching into slight hollows left from the preparatory planes. The proportion of plane length to blade width used in full-size planes can also be scaled down to the smaller planes used in smaller-scale work.

AND REMEMBER…

There is an additional aspect of effective plane work that tends to be overlooked—the sharpness of the blade. No planing operation will be very effective unless the blade is sharp. This becomes unavoidably apparent during demanding finish-planing operations. While you can continue to push a dull plane with increasing effort and increasing tearout when roughing down a board (the change is so gradual, the blade often is dull before you notice it), on a demanding finish-planing operation, unless the plane is exquisitely sharp, results will be immediately disappointing—no waiting.

Beginners often find sharpness difficult to judge. It is often a fleeting thing, seemingly there one moment and gone the next. As your wookworking skills grow, you will become more demanding of your tools and accept only true sharpness. You will learn that some blades do not get as sharp as others. There are nuances of difference in the concept of sharp. Without a blade sharp enough for the task, however, all other strategies for effective planing fail. I think you will find, at least in the better Japanese blades, a depth of capability that you will find yourself spending the better part of your woodworking career trying to find the end of.

3

TRADITIONAL TECHNIQUES

The Jack, Jointer, and Smoothing Planes

In both the East and the West, handplanes perform three basic functions

in woodworking: shaping and dimensioning lumber, truing and preparing

pieces for gluing, and smoothing surfaces. The correct application of the

anatomical tactics discussed in Chapter 2 is critical to effectively performing

these tasks. Because each task requires a significantly different combination

of tactics, traditionally a different plane was developed and used for each: in

the West these planes are called the jack, the jointer, and the smoothing plane,

respectively (and I will refer to the Japanese counterparts by the Western name

according to their function). They are visually distinguished from each other

primarily by their length relative to the width of their blade, and by the shape

of the blade's edge. Varying other tactics as well maximizes work efficiency.

Three Japanese planes. From left a jack plane, a jointer plane, and a smoothing plane.

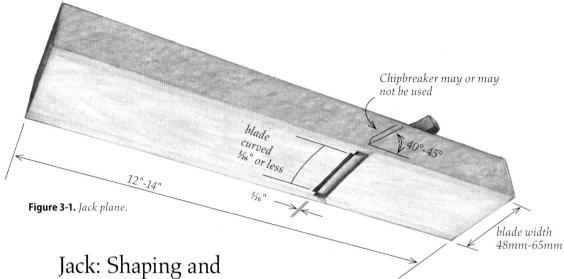

Chipbreaker may or may
not be used

blade
curved
1/16" or less

40°–45°

12"–14"

1/16"

blade width
48mm–65mm

Figure 3-1. *Jack plane.*

Jack: Shaping and Dimensioning

Most closely identified with shaping and dimensioning lumber is, what is called in the West, the jack plane. It is traditionally used to remove a fair amount of wood quickly to bring a piece to rough shape and dimension after being rough-sawn, split, or hewn from the log. The Japanese version is usually is about 14" (350mm) long (roughly the same length as its Western counterpart), this slightly longer length aiding in the initial straightening and leveling of stock from the rough. For rapid stock removal, and to reduce tearout and resistance, the edge of the blade is sharpened to a curve, projecting around 1/16" (1mm), or less, depending on the judgment of the woodworker (Figure 3-2).

The chipbreaker, if used, is set well back

from the edge a 1/16" (2mm) or less. In addition, to minimize effort in using the plane, the blade is narrow, about 1¾" (48mm) up to 2½" (65mm). The blade angle is set at 40°, though if working hardwoods the blade could be set at 43° to 45°. The sole is configured with the contact area behind the blade relieved perhaps 0.02" (0.5mm) more or less. Because this is a rough plane and makes a deep cut, maintenance of a flat bottom is less critical.

Though it may vary from trade to trade and region to region, it is common for the carpenter to use more than one jack or preparatory plane when preparing stock. The first plane might be a little shorter (or not) and narrower, 60mm or less, but would be a single blade plane (i.e. without a chipbreaker) to facilitate removing large amounts of wood. A 14" (350mm) jack with a chipbreaker and a straighter blade edge would follow this. This would be used to further refine the surface and eliminate some of the tearout left by the first plane. The jointer, or truing, plane would follow this.

Figure 3-2. *Jack plane mouth opening.*

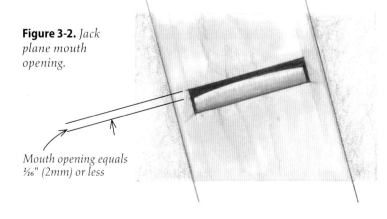

Mouth opening equals
1/16" (2mm) or less

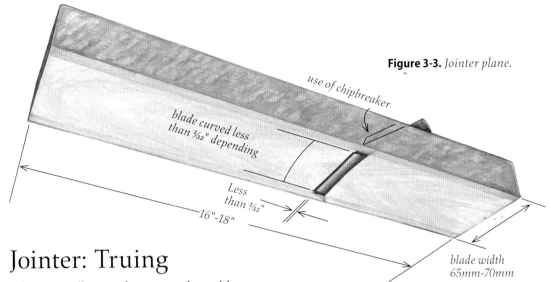

Figure 3-3. *Jointer plane.*

use of chipbreaker

blade curved less than 1/32" depending

Less than 1/32"

16"-18"

blade width 65mm-70mm

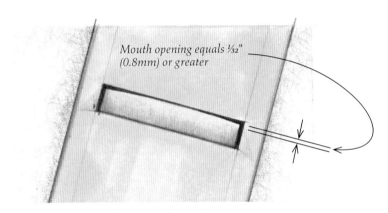

Mouth opening equals 1/32" (0.8mm) or greater

Figure 3-4. *Jointer plane mouth opening.*

Jointer: Truing

After generally straightening and roughly dimensioning the stock with the jack, the jointer—a long, wide plane—is used to remove the roughness left by the jack and to true surfaces and edges in preparation for final smoothing. The Japanese jointer generally is shorter than that used in the West, 16" to 18" long. Its longer length and greater width—the blade is usually 2½" (65mm) but more likely 2¾" (70mm) wide—results in a flat surface overall. Its wide blade, honed straight with the corners lightly dubbed off or with a very slight curve, takes out the ridges left by the more coarsely set jack, and aids in truing faces and edges of boards. The chipbreaker is set back from the blade edge only the distance of the thickest shaving being cut. When used to work hardwood, I suggest a cutting angle of 43° to 47½°, though, generally, unless you make your own you will find them with a 40° blade angle. The sole is trued dead flat and as is typical, relieved slightly in strategic places to simplify keeping it true.

A craftsman will often have two of these truing planes, the second one more of a smoother, or panel plane, than what we might call a jointer. The blade will be a little straighter, the throat smaller, the blade better, and the bottom flatter than the first plane. This sets up the work for the smoothing planes to follow (Figure 3-4).

Additionally, a plane made specifically for jointing edges, as well as faces, is made. When used to plane edges, this plane is used on its edge, much as in the West edges are shot on a shooting board. For this reason, its right side is thicker to accommodate the loss of material there as that side is trued and squared to the sole during regular maintenance. I don't know if a left hand version is made. The plane is also used for face jointing before the smoothing plane is used.

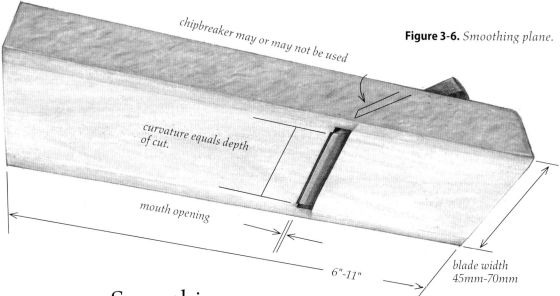

chipbreaker may or may not be used

Figure 3-6. *Smoothing plane.*

curvature equals depth of cut.

mouth opening

6"-11"

blade width 45mm-70mm

Smoothing

The smoothing plane, in the full size planes to match the 18" jointers, has blade widths from 55mm to 2¾" (70mm), or even greater, with the length of the plane being a little greater than three times the block width or around 10" to 11"-plus long for a 70mm plane. Japanese craftsmen seem to prefer wider planes for their work overall, with 70mm (2¾") being a not uncommon width (I don't think there's even a 2¾"-wide smoothing plane in production in the West). Whether this is a result of the indigenous

woods they use being softer and thus easier to cut, or because it gives a better surface with less variation from the sweep of the blade, is hard to say.

The sequence for the final smoothing of wood is a bit different than what a Western woodworker might be used to, but it is highly efficient and productive, and should be considered as a method of work no matter what style of plane you use. At all stages the sweep of the blade is finer, with less curvature than what we might use in the West. A finely set and longer truing plane is used first, of the jointer size as discussed in the previous section, leaving a surface very flat with few defects. This sets up the work for the smoothing plane, allowing it to be finely set to remove all tearout (Figure 3-8). But instead of a single smoothing plane, a craftsman will have two, but probably three smoothing planes, each one set up finer than the last, each having a better blade than the last. If the surface is satisfactory after the first

Figure 3-5. *Japanese-style jointers: 70mm (2¾") blade with a 40° pitch (left); 70mm (2¾") blade with a 47½° pitch (right), both 16" (450mm) long.*

smoother, fine. But if the wood is difficult, or the surface not to the craftsman liking, it will be worked by the second, more finely set plane, and the third, best plane, if necessary (Figure 3-9).

This is a far more productive method than using a single plane and resetting the depth of cut, chipbreaker, and mouth opening—and resharpening—as the work progresses. This is especially true as you are only going to get really good results if the blade is freshly sharpened. In addition, to get the finest surface, there must be a progression to the curve of the blades used and possibly in the shape of the sole. It's too big a step to go from the curve of a jointer plane blade to that of a plane that is going to give you a really flat, polished surface, as the plane will be too finely set to actually plane much material. If only using one plane, at the very least you would have to change out blades for a straighter one as the work progresses or resharpen to shape. Having planes dedicated to different levels of fineness makes the work go quicker (Figure 3-10).

It's not unusual for a woodworker's finest plane to be single bladed—without a chipbreaker—relying solely on the sharpness of the blade to produce stunning results. As well, depending on the finish and wood, a craftsman may use a plane with a lower cutting angle, with or without a chipbreaker, to give a cleaner shear for the final surface.

Of course, planes smaller than 65mm (2½") and 70mm (3") can be used, most especially for smaller work, or general use,

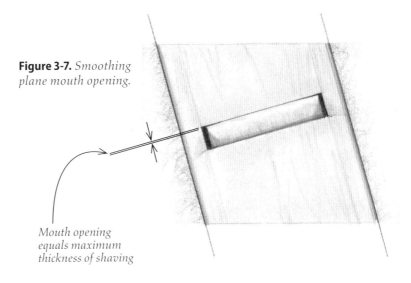

Figure 3-7. *Smoothing plane mouth opening.*

Mouth opening equals maximum thickness of shaving

Figure 3-8. *For larger surfaces, on hardwood, I may use this 16" (40.6cm)-long panel plane, left, with a 70mm (2¾")-wide blade bedded at 47½°. I may follow it with the 11" (27.9cm) smoother with a 70mm blade at 47½°, right, or one of the coffin-sided smoothers.*

much like you would use the Stanley #60½ block plane. These are a joy to use and are far easier to master than the 70mm planes. I suggest you start with one of these and learn on it, before graduating to the bigger planes. And of course your whole sequence of planes can be smaller, especially if you are working hardwoods. Note that the Western smoothing plane is often only 48mm wide.

Figure 3-9. *This is one of my favorite combinations. The 70mm (2¾")
plane, bottom, has a blade bedded at 40° and is one of my most used
planes. I often follow it with the plane in the center, which has a 70mm
(2¾") blade at 43°. If the surface still needs work, I may use the plane at
top, which has a very nice 70mm (2¾") blade at 45°.*

And it is to be noted that the Japanese style
of plane is easily modified. It is especially
useful to have planes whose length to
width ratio is greatly reduced to allow the
very finely set blade of the final smoother
to access to the surface. The converse of
the functional shape of the jointer plane
applies: while the length of the jointer trues
a surface by bridging the hills and valleys, a
very short plane will smooth the surface by
following them.

As well, if you get in the habit of making
your own planes, you can also easily make
planes with different blade angles than
commonly available.

JACK VARIATIONS

Strictly speaking nowadays, any plane used for roughing out stock could be called a jack plane. For instance, I have a
couple of small planes, both Japanese, which I use for shaping. The coarsest one has a blade 1¼" (32mm) wide and is
about 8" (203mm) long. Because I use this for smaller and narrower pieces, the blade is rather straight across its width, but
the sole of the plane is shaped to a slight curve. The slight curve allows me to use it to shape pieces with a long sweep, or
simply to get in there and remove a lot of stock without it bridging the low spots. The throat is large. The second plane is
slightly wider, about the same length as the first and flat on the bottom. I use the second plane to shape mostly flat stock,
or perhaps experiment with a convex curve or twist in a piece. I also often use this one to shape convex curves and have
since fitted an adjustable block on the end to assist in this.

Figure 3-10. *These three planes all have a 70mm (2 ¾") blade set at 40°, great for planing softwood. I use the 16" (406mm)-long plane, left, as a panel plane to prepare the surface for the plane in the center to smooth. If the wood is particularly difficult, I may finish with the plane at right, which has a very high-quality blade.*

THE IDEAL EDGE SHAPE

Ideally, the edge of a smoothing plane should be straight across, with the ends tapered off to avoid leaving tracks in the work. The taper needs to equal the depth of cut, which may be less than 0.005" (.13mm). This is most easily achieved by added pressure at each corner when sharpening: five strokes for each corner on the first sharpening stone (in addition to sharpening the main edge), a few more than that on the finishing stone(s) can be enough. The resulting configuration works well, but I could not swear that it looks like the drawing.

PLANES FOR JOINERY

There exist quite a variety of joinery planes in the Japanese lexicon. Most of these are trade specific such as a spectrum of V-cutting planes used by *shoji* makers to cut grooves across *kumiko*, (the lattice sticks onto which the paper of shoji doors is glued), so that they can be folded to make elaborate flower patterns. And many trades have size-specific grooving and dado planes, as well as adjustable ones.

The ones I find most valuable are the two types of rabbet planes, the moving fillister plane, and two styles of side-rabbet planes.

*Japanese skewed-blade
rabbet planes.*

Rabbet Planes

A rabbet plane is any plane whose blade projects to the edge of the sole on one or both sides of the plane. This allows it to cut right into the corner of a stepped cut—called a rabbet (also, a rebate)—something a bench plane cannot do. Besides the basic rabbet plane (which does not have a fence), there is also the fillister plane (a rabbet plane with a fixed fence), and the moving-fillister plane (a rabbet plane with an adjustable fence).

The Japanese have two basic forms of the rabbet plane. One form has the blade flush with both sides of the plane; this is nearly identical to the Western version, with one exception. The second type is "handed," left or right, and has a skewed blade and sometimes a nicker.

SHOULDERED BLADE RABBET PLANES

The first type of rabbet planet is about the same size and same general concept as its Western counterpart. The main difference here, though it makes little difference to the functioning of the plane, is that, unlike any of the bench planes, the chipbreaker is

the wedge for the blade. This means that chipbreaker must be fitted so that as it reaches full pressure on the blade, it is just coming to its proper setting at the edge of the blade. Tricky.

The shouldered, or T-shaped blade is several times thicker than the shouldered blade used in a Western rabbet plane (about 9mm), and is tapered, the blade portion being thicker than the top (see Chapter 6). This is to allow the blade to be withdrawn through the mouth. The chipbreaker is also tapered, though in the opposite direction, thicker at the top to form a wedge. The blade is bedded usually at 40° or less; an antique I have has its bladed bedded at around 43½° or 9 in 10.

The back of the blade is flat only for the width of the shank above it. It then flares up to its full width. The blade bed reflects this and is probably meant to support the sides of the blade, though at some point some lateral adjustment will have to take place, reducing its effectiveness at resisting any tendency to twist under load.

The plane is meant to be pulled, as with any other Japanese plane, so the blade is set further back than its Western counterparts to accommodate this. It can, of course, be pushed as well (just don't tell anyone!).

The advantage of the Japanese version of this type of rabbet plane is the superior steel, and a hardened, functioning chipbreaker, which when combined, can virtually eliminate tearout, or be quickly readjusted to hog off large amounts of wood.

There is a wide version of this plane, lower, but with a wide shouldered-blade (Figure

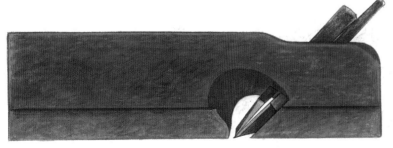

Figure 4-1. *The Japanese rabbet plane is very similar to the Western form, differing only in the relative placement of the blade along the length of the plane, and the use of a chipbreaker both to improve the cut and to wedge the blade. The blade and chipbreaker are both laminated steel.*

4-2). The blade and chipbreaker function in the same manner as its narrower cousin.

SKEWED BLADE RABBET PLANES

A rabbet plane is often used across the grain—to pare the thickness of a tenon or a tongue, for instance. A skewed blade works at an angle to the grain, rather than perpendicular to it, resulting in a much smoother cut. It also can be used to form or to smooth the field on a door panel (two of the four fielding cuts on a panel are cross grain), a cut that will show and must be smooth. A blade cutting directly perpendicular to the grain will tear the surface. The skewed blade also can hog off more wood with or across the grain, with less resistance, than a blade bedded perpendicular. The drawback is that these planes rarely come with cutters wider than around 1 ¼" (32mm). If you consistently do larger work, then accuracy in trimming is strained by having to make repeated overlapping passes. Another difficulty can be encountered if you work with tropical hardwoods, as the efficacy of a skewed blade is lost on these woods when cutting with the grain, though it still cuts superbly across the grain.

The skew blade rabbet plane, unlike the shoulder blade rabbet plane, functions like the bench planes with a wedge shaped blade fitted into matching escapements, the chipbreaker held by a pin and operating independent of the blade. The blade mount is skewed in two directions in order to get the point of the blade directly into the corner of

Figure 4-2. *An uncommon Japanese rabbet plane with a full width 2 ¾" (70mm) blade. Like its narrower shouldered-blade rabbet plane, but unlike the smoothing planes, the chipbreaker also forms the wedge that secures the blade. The plane is narrow on top to give hand clearance when working up against a deep shoulder.*

Figure 4-3. *A pair of Japanese skewed-blade rabbet planes.*

the rabbet, and is bedded with around a 40° or less cutting angle (mine are around 38°). (For setting up and tuning the rabbet plane, see "Rabbet Planes" on page 46.)

SKEWED BLADE MOVING FILLISTER PLANES

There are moving fillister versions of the skew blade rabbet plane. These are basically the same plane with the addition of a scoring spur, dovetailed in section, tapered in length

USING THE FILLISTER PLANE

When the using any rabbet plane, initially adjust the blade slightly less than 1/64" (.4mm) beyond the side of the plane, even though this appears to put it beyond the edge of the spur (see illustration at right). Surprisingly, this usually works. If the cut is tearing up beyond the score line, then the blade is protruding too much and must be backed off. If the plane steps away from the score line as the cut proceeds, then the blade needs to protrude more. Experiment with your set-ups before proceeding to the work so you know how your plane is behaving.

Measure the width of the rabbet from the spur—which essentially is the side of the plane (not the edge of the blade). Measure at each fixing point of the fence to ensure that the fence is parallel to the sole.

When making a cross-grain rabbet with a fillister plane, draw the plane backward at least once to get a clean score line that completely cuts the top fibers. Make sure the fence is in solid contact with the work when you do this, because it is easy to tilt the plane, and end up scoring a line beyond the rabbet, and mar the work.

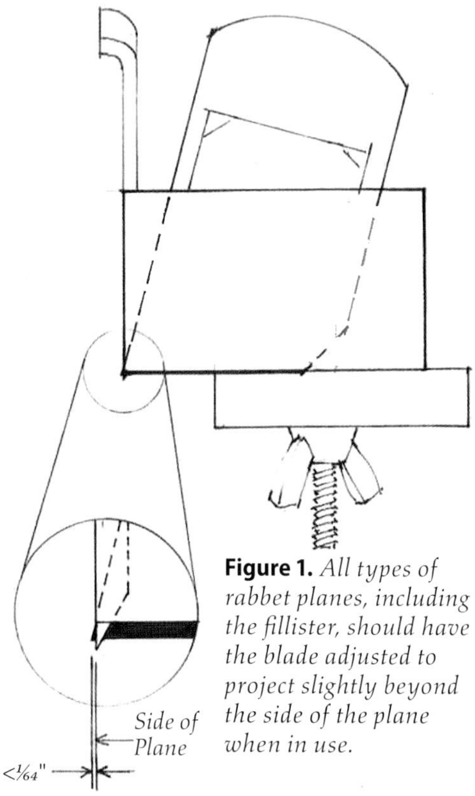

If you find your rabbet has stepped out after you have cut it, you have a couple options. If you are not too far along, you can readjust the blade to where it should have been (projecting 1/64", or .4mm),

Figure 1. *All types of rabbet planes, including the fillister, should have the blade adjusted to project slightly beyond the side of the plane when in use.*

Side of Plane

<1/64"

and then, keeping the fence tightly on the work, take repeated light cuts. The point of the blade will just cut into the work removing what it should have the first time. It is a bit frustrating, but often the most accurate way if you can keep the fence on the work. Also, check the alignment of the fence. If it is not parallel to the sole, it can hold the plane off the line. Measure at both fixing points and reset as necessary.

Alternatively, you can correct a stepped out rabbet by turning the plane on its side and squaring up the shoulder of the rabbet. You can reset the fence so it does not exceed the score line or just eyeball it to the score line. If you did not reset the blade before you started this, however, the blade will step out in the other direction, resulting in a mess remaining in the corner. Then you will have to use the first technique—even more difficult when you get to this point. On occasion, it may be easier to clean up the shoulder with a side-rabbet plane, but make sure the point does not set below the bottom of the plane or you will repeatedly score the rabbet, and the plane will resist cutting sideways.

and inlaid into the side of the plane in line with the point of the blade; and a moveable fence fixed by wing nuts. The wings of these are sometimes are in the way when the maximum width of cut is set. In this case you will have to rotate the screws until the wing nut can be tightened down out of the way.

Side-rabbet Planes

The Japanese side-rabbet plane comes in a few different sizes and two different methods of holding the blade. The smallest versions have the single blade self-wedge into the side of the plane; this type can also be found in the larger sizes. The other type of side-rabbet plane has a chipbreaker that, unlike most other Japanese planes, doubles as the wedge that holds the blade in position (functionally similar to the shouldered blade rabbet plane). This means that the chipbreaker must be tapped down close to its final position before you can begin adjusting the blade. If the chipbreaker is not tapped into position, the blade is liable to come flying out at the first disturbance, injuring you, or the blade, or both. Despite this, I like this tool. It is easy to hold, easy to use and adjust, has a high-quality laminated blade with a chipbreaker (sometimes tearout on the side of a groove is not acceptable), and it can be modified. I angled the adjacent face of mine to the angle of the dovetail plane I have. The angle allows the plane to fit right to the bottom corner of the dovetail grove, and gives me a decent reference face to assist in holding the plane at the correct angle. As with the other side-rabbet planes, if you are not going to take the time to back up the wood when the plane exits a cross-grain cut, you really need a right- and left-hand model. Otherwise, you risk splitting out the wood.

Figure 4-4. *A Japanese moving-fillister plane with a chipbreaker, scoring knife or spur, and a brass sole plate to reduce wear. The plane is a solid performer, able to remove large amounts of wood or to be set finely to leave a polished cut. It can also be used across the grain. It has a few idiosyncrasies, however: the maximum width of cut is only 1" (25mm) and at its maximum setting, the wing nuts that tighten the fence can interfere with the work. Remedy the problem by reinstalling their screws so the wing nuts tighten down in an out-of-the-way position. As with many rabbet planes, the chips will pack in the opening right above the blade point. Open the area with a file.*

Figure 4-5 *The two types of side rabbet planes, used for trimming or smoothing the sides of grooves, dados and rabbets. These come handed like the skewed-blade rabbet planes. The plane in the background has a chipbreaker, used to wedge the blade, and the plane in the foreground has a single self-wedging blade.*

5

PLANES FOR SHAPING WOOD

Compass planes, spoonbottom planes, hollowing and rounding planes, different types of chamfering planes, and miniature planes for fairing curves: Unlike their Western counterparts, the Japanese still produce a variety of planes for shaping wood. They are comfortable to use, easy to control, and also ideal for modifying to exactly fit the shape you are trying to produce.

A Japanese-style compass plane, its sole shaped to a gentle curve, smoothes the sweep of a bench seat.

Figure 5-1. *A collection of Japanese-style compass planes in different sweeps.*

Figure 5-2. *The adjustable nose on this Japanese plane enables it to perform like a compass plane for a limited range of convex surfaces.*

WESTERN VERSUS JAPANESE PLANES FOR CURVES

Getting a good reference on the plane when starting and finishing a stroke is important.

I find most Western-style planes with their short nose (sole in front of the blade) difficult to start on a curve. This short nose is typically only one-third of the overall length of the plane. This is one of the reasons I prefer the Japanese-style plane for curves. Its blade position, about three-fifths of the overall length from the front, makes it a little easier to start. If you make a compass plane from scratch, proportion it so the blade is closer to the center of the length of the sole; this way, you will have good reference coming on and going off the piece.

Compass Planes

The sole of a compass plane (Figure 5-1) curves along its length, either convex or (less commonly) concave. Few compass planes are manufactured today in the West. However, the Japanese still make a few compass planes and they are easily modified to different curves. I have modified small (usually about 45mm wide) Japanese-style planes into convex-soled compass planes. I prefer the Japanese-style plane for this because I find that pulling the plane, combined with its low position and more central blade, gives me a lot of control.

Compass planes are most useful when the work is concave. Strictly speaking, the plane should match the radius of the piece being worked, but in reality, the radius of the plane (on concave work) need be only no larger than that of the work. Nevertheless, the closer the two match, the easier it is to get good results. (See Chapter 9 for Making a Compass Plane.)

A convex curve can be worked with a straight (bench) plane—the plane does not have to be curved at all. For this reason, I have no planes with soles that are concave in length. I now have a plane with a nosepiece that adjusts up and down that has given satisfactory results on a variety of work (Figure 5-2).

If you like to experiment with shapes, you may find it useful to have a plane or two of a size that matches the scale of your work for rough shaping. I have a couple of

USING A COMPASS PLANE

When fairing a curve along the length of a somewhat narrow piece, whether convex or concave, use the compass plane to remove the obvious high spots first to get a relatively smooth-flowing curve. Then concentrate on the beginning of the stroke and the finish. These are the areas of greatest difficulty.

The most common mistake is to dip the plane on entry and exit from the stroke causing unevenness at one or both ends. It is all the more difficult because the curve of your plane will almost never be exactly that of your piece. This means you have to rock the plane slightly until you find the sweet spot—the position where the blade contacts the work and begins to cut—and maintain this position through the whole cut.

Maintaining the position is relatively easy once you have found it. The problem is that you often do not find it until after you have begun the cut, and you just as often lose it before finishing the cut, resulting in the very ends being uneven. Concentrate and find the position at the very start, before you begin the cut, and maintain it as you exit the piece. This requires putting pressure on the front of the plane when starting the cut, and shifting the pressure to the back of the plane when finishing.

If the piece is convex, I begin with a bench plane, usually a coarsely set smooth plane, to take the high spots out. I skew the plane to the downhill side to get more of a shearing cut so there is less tearing, rather than using it straight across. Once the overall curve is even, I begin smoothing the curve with the compass plane **(Figure 1)**.

To fair a concave curve along the length of a wide piece, I often work cross grain first

Figure 1. *To fair a concave curve along the length of a wide piece, I often work cross-grain first with a large-radius hollowing plane (the sole being convex in width) to take out the high spots and begin evening the curve.*

Figure 2. *Then I will work with the grain with the compass plane. If there is considerable variation in the surface I may use a plane with a smaller radius to knock down the high spots, switching to a plane whose curve is a close match to the curve to even the sweep. To finish smoothing I may switch again to a plane with a slightly smaller radius much as you would finish with a short smoothing plane after preparing the surface with a longer panel plane or jointer plane.*

Figure 3. *Because the radius of the compass plane is often slightly less than the radius of the piece being worked (it must be no larger than that of the work), you may have to lift the front of the plane slightly to get a good start. Otherwise, the plane will start cutting after you have begun the stroke, not from the very beginning, resulting in an uneven curve at the end.*

USING A COMPASS PLANE *(continued)*

with a large-radius hollowing plane (the sole being convex in width) to even up the curve, taking out the high spots **(Figure 2)**. Then I'll work along the grain with the compass plane, sometimes using a plane of a slightly smaller radius to first knock down the ridges left by the cross grain planning **(Figure 3)**. The start and finish of the long stroke on a wide piece presents the same problem (and solution) here as on a narrow piece **(Figure 4)**.

Next to the start and finish in fairing a curve, the point where the grain changes direction on the curve of the piece is the most difficult, whether the piece is convex or concave. The best you can do, after you have established a satisfactory curve, is to re-sharpen if necessary, back the blade off to make the thinnest of cuts, and adjust the chipbreaker down tight to the blade edge. Work just to where the grain changes, and then come back from the other direction, overlapping slightly so you do not end up with a hump but rather a smooth continuous curve **(Figure 5)**. Hopefully, your adjustments will reduce the tear-out to a tolerable level. Finish with a scraper shave, sometimes called a chairmaker's scraper, if you have one, and a card scraper until the tear-out is removed. Remember to work the whole surface, or you will destroy the evenness of your curve. Finally, you can even out any remaining irregularities, if necessary, by using a sanding block made from a scrap band sawn to the curve of the piece. I always save these sanding blocks (I have a box full) to save me the effort on any similar curves I encounter in the future.

One final note: When starting a convex curve, back the blade off a little more than you might think. Because the convex curve

Figure 4. *If the piece is convex, I begin with a bench plane, usually a coarsely set smooth plane, to take off the high spots. Then I use a compass plane, in this case a straight-soled plane with an adjustable nose, to smooth the curve.*

Figure 5. *To avoid a hump in a curve where the grain changes, work with a re-sharpened blade set for a thin cut and with the chipbreaker set tight to the edge. Overlap the grain change slightly.*

of the work projects *into* the mouth of the plane, the cut will be deeper than it appears it should be when sighting down the plane.

small Japanese planes that I use to form long sweeps, for instance (Figure 5-3).

Additionally, I have built up a collection, project by project, of small compass planes in various radii (Figure 5-4). Some of these I bought, some I shaped from small planes I bought for the purpose. I have been able to tune these planes to get good, finished surfaces from them.

Hollows and Rounds

The Japanese make planes for rounding and hollowing in various sizes and radii, though an extensive selection is hard to find. These differ from the Western version in that they usually have chipbreakers and are bedded with a 40° cutting angle. The functioning is the same as with the bench planes with the wedge shaped blade fitting into matching escapements and the chipbreaker held by a crosspin.

While the chipbreaker is useful for reducing tearout, the low angle encourages tearout in some hardwoods. It takes some fastidious setup to eliminate tearout. The curve of the sole, blade, and chipbreaker must be near perfect matches, with the blade actually being a slightly smaller radius so the corners of the blade flush up with the sole, much as you would dub off the corners of a smoothing plane. As well, the sole must be trued in both its length and its radius in order to get the finest tearout-free cut, considerably more difficult than on a flat surface. I have to admit I use them only occasionally, so I have not invested the time to prepare them for

Figure 5-3. *I added an adjustable nosepiece to the plane at left to aid in shaping convex curves.*

Figure 5-4. *This collection of small compass planes I have made or purchased over the years.*

THE CORRECT SOLE CONFIGURATION

For best results if the piece is concave, the radius of the plane should be equal to or slightly smaller than that of the piece; if the piece is convex, the radius of the plane should be equal to or slight larger. However, even a straight-soled plane can shape a convex curve.

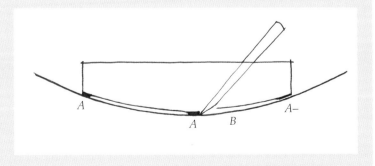

the finest work. I often use them for rough or first shaping. But I like them; they're comfortable and generally quite effective. When I have a curve to do I reach for them first.

Using the planes is relatively straightforward. The hollowing plane is easiest to start in a machine-made hollow, at least a rough concavity. If starting a hollow from scratch, you can clamp a fence to the plane, but oftentimes it is just as easy to use your fingers as a fence. Start with the chipbreaker backed off. After a few strokes,

Figure 5-5. *An unmatched set of hollows and rounds in the Japanese style, bought as needed.*

HOLLOWS & ROUNDS

There is some confusion in the nomenclature of hollows and rounds, probably arising out of colloquial traditions, or perhaps due to the near interchangeability of the terms hollow and hollowing, and round and rounding. Often the terms hollow and round will refer to the shape of the planes themselves, rather than the shapes they cut. Thus, a round plane will make a hollowing cut, and a hollow plane will make a rounding cut. Generally, I use hollowing plane to mean a plane that cuts a hollow, having a convex blade; a rounding plane is a plane that rounds a piece over and has a concave blade. I hope that clears that up!

the hollow is self-jigging (though you can pop out of it if you don't pay attention). For hollows wider than the blade, you tilt the plane to work the side of the hollow, changing the tilt after each stroke as you work your way across. As the work progresses retract the blade for a finer cut and set the chipbreaker down closer to the edge to reduce tearout. Chances are the blade radius will not exactly match that of the hollow, so you will have to follow up with a curved scraper to fair out the blade marks.

With a rounding plane, it is best to form most of the round with a steel-bottom plane or spokeshave, to save wear and tear on the wood-soled rounding plane. You can also set the bench plane or spokeshave for a deeper cut to speed the work and finish with light cuts of the rounding plane. Again, chances are the radius of the blade will not exactly match that of the work, so you can fair the blade marks with a thin flexible scraper or a scraper ground to the curve. (For setting up hollows and rounds, see "Setting up Hollows and Rounds" on page 91.)

Other Shaping Planes

Here are some more useful planes, though your use of them will depend on the type and style of work you like to do. For instance, think about the kind of treatment you give the edges of your pieces: this treatment can affect the look and feel of the piece—perhaps soft, with a rounded chamfer, or maybe hard, with the extra shadow line of a beveled chamfer making the piece appear lighter or thinner. The way you approach this feature can become a signature. Chamfer planes can be useful and efficient tools for forming these edges.

Woodworkers involved in more sculptural shaping of wood—one-of-a-kind furniture-makers, chair makers, reproduction furniture makers, woodcarvers, instrument makers, and the woodworker making prototypes for pieces to be put into production—will find the compass planes and *chibi kanna* (little planes) indispensable for successfully forming and smoothing sweeping shapes.

CHAMFER PLANES

Chamfer planes (Figure 5-6) are a useful addition to most tool kits. When it would take too much time to set up the router for a short run, or the work is too awkward or difficult to access, these are the tools to use to finish an edge. They have the added advantage of leaving a surface that may need little or no further smoothing.

While you can use a block plane or a rounding plane to chamfer an edge, the advantage of a chamfer plane is that its fences give quicker, more accurate, and repeatable results. The Japanese are big users of chamfer planes and are one of the best sources (if not the only source) of reliable edge forming planes. They do make some cheaper versions of the tool without chipbreakers, but the best tools will have a matching chipbreaker and a laminated blade.

One of my favorite tools is the 45° straight chamfer plane (also available in a 30°–60° chamfer). This is a small plane captured between its angled fences so that it can move

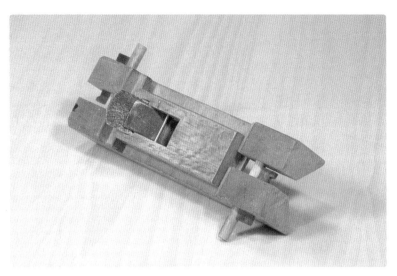

Figure 5-6. *A homemade Japanese-style chamfer plane. Small rabbets were cut on each end of a purchased plane to capture it in the carriage/ fence assembly. The width of the chamfer is fixed by tightening wedges on the cross dowels.*

Figure 5-7. *An adjustable Japanese chamfer plane for forming 45° chamfers. This plane has a slightly skewed blade, which is preferable as it allows it to be used on an end-grain chamfer. The plane itself, captured by rabbets both ends, can be moved left or right in the carriage/fence assembly to extend the wear from narrow chamfers across the full width of the blade; and the plane has a brass piece let into the sole at the mouth to reduce wear. These are also available in 60°/30° chamfer configurations.*

in its carriage side to side, thus spreading the wear of the narrow sharp edge of the wood across the full width of the blade, extending the time between sharpenings. The width of the chamfer is also adjustable. This plane

Figure 5-8. *A Japanese chamfer plane for forming ⅛" (3mm) diameter roundovers. The back underside has been cut away to allow greater access to inside corners.*

Figure 5-9. *An adjustable Japanese chamfer plane for forming ⅜" (10mm) diameter roundovers. This plane has adjustable fences on either side, allowing three types of cut: a simple roundover, a roundover with a single shoulder or bead, and a roundover with a shoulder on either side.*

BLOCK PLANE, THEN CHAMFER

To speed the work, you can use a coarsely set block plane, like a Stanley #60 ½, to rough down a chamfer, especially if it is a big one, and then finish up with a finely set chamfer plane for a smooth edge. This process is usually not only faster but saves wear and tear on the chamfer or roundover plane, which has a wood sole.

comes in two versions: one with the blade mounted perpendicular to the stroke of the plane, and another with the blade skewed roughly 20°. This last version can also be found in right and left hand versions. If you can, get the skewed version. This will allow you to chamfer cross-grain as well, as the skew—when oriented properly—will shear on the bias, making a much cleaner cut than a perpendicular blade (Figure 5-7).

My other favorite tool (hard to say which one I use more!) is the rounded-edge chamfer plane. The small version I have forms about a ⅛" (3mm) roundover, perfect for taking the sharpness off an edge and making it hand-friendly (Figure 5-8). The fences on this are fixed, but the main difference between this plane and its many East and West versions is that it has a chipbreaker, which can be set down close to the edge to eliminate tearout: faster than a router and the results often don't have to be sanded. Additionally, the back has been cut away to allow the plane to get in close on inside corners.

I have a larger version of the round chamfer plane, which forms a ³⁄₁₆" (5mm) diameter chamfer and has adjustable fences. This allows it to produce three different profiles: a roundover, roundover with a shoulder, and a roundover with a shoulder both sides. This plane also has a chipbreaker (Figure 5-9).

SPOONBOTTOM PLANES

A spoonbottom plane (Figure 5-10) curves both along and across its sole, giving it a shape somewhat like, well, a spoon's bottom.

Most often, they are used for the shaping stage of work rather than final smoothing because of the difficulty of matching the blade and plane curvature rather exactly to the work, especially when the radius is constantly changing such as in a chair seat. A number of these are needed if they are to be used for smoothing and transitioning complex curves. Since there are a limited number of radii available, you will probably have to make these yourself, either from a small plane, or if the blade curvature is severe, from scratch. (See "Hollowing, Rounding, and Spoonbottom Planes" on page 136.)

Smallish planes (around 4", or 102mm, long) that can be used with two hands are the least fatiguing and most effective for heavy work. Surprisingly, the boxy form of the Japanese plane is quite easy and comfortable to cup in both hands (may take a little rounding of the *dai* though), giving great power and control.

In use, the spoonbottom plane is often an intermediate step in the production of a smooth form. Traditionally, for instance, a shape such as a chair seat would first be roughed out with an adze. In some cases, this might be followed by the spoonbottom plane, but more likely the form would be further refined with an inshave and then a travisher, which is a wood spokeshave with a curved blade. Much like spoonbottom planes, these come in a variety of curvatures to fair out the changing curves. Inshaves and travishers are prone to tearout, and when used across the grain as well as with it, and leaving a

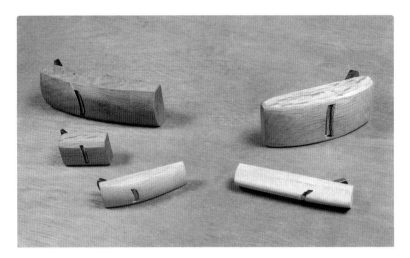

Figure 5-10. *Spoonbottom planes.*

rough surface. The results are clean up with the spoonbottom plane. Having a number of these with different radii is helpful to get into all the areas and not only ease the transitions, but smooth the surface. Remove the light rippling left by the curve of the blade with a series of curved-edge and flexible scrapers.

LITTLE PLANES: *CHIBI KANNA*

These are little Japanese-style planes usually no longer than 2" (51mm). Used to shape wood, they are made by each woodworker to whatever blade shape and sole configuration he might need. Many Japanese woodworkers will have a box of them, made over the years for specific projects. They are what the Westerner might call finger planes, or instrument-maker planes, and I have found them to be very useful. They are quick to make and highly effective for getting into all sorts of areas to shape, fair, or smooth some of the more sculptural aspects of a design. Any woodworker whose projects involve curving surfaces of any kind should have a number of these.

Figure 5-11. *A small collection of chibi-kanna. The plane at the top of the photo is used for planing small strips to the same thickness.*

Figure 5-12 *A piece of the blade stock for making chibi-kanna, a bit smaller than it was as purchased, since a couple of blades have been made from it; and a couple of pieces of Japanese white oak for making the dai saved from the cut-off of a larger plane block.*

Traditionally, the blade stock for the *chibi kanna* (Figure 5-12) comes in about 4" (102mm)-wide sections (the blade length is about 2", or 51mm). This is a laminated piece of steel, like the material out of which the bigger blades are made and is available in different grades. To make a blade, you cut its required width off this 4" (102mm) blank. (See "Making *Chibi Kanna*" on page 131.) Making a blade this way gives the craftsman a great deal of flexibility in the width of blade and blade shape he can have. This blade stock is hard to find now (it never was easy to come by), but precut blades of different widths are still available, making the fabrication of these small planes a viable option.

Fabricating these small planes is the same as for the larger ones, but since the blades are usually only ½" to 1" (13mm to 25mm) wide and are not usually fitted with a chipbreaker (which takes extra time to fit), they can be made quickly. In addition, since you do not have to wait for any glue to dry, you can use them right away. I usually make the blade angle 43° (9 in 10) unless I am working some particularly hard woods, in which case I increase the pitch.

SETTING UP JAPANESE PLANES

Nearly everything about the Japanese plane is different from what you know about Western planes. The tactics of the anatomy are the same, but solutions to the mechanics are different and highly refined.

The handplane is unmatched in its ability to get a crisp, clean, clear surface on wood.

If you are not familiar with setting up and using a Japanese plane, I suggest starting out with a 45mm to 48mm (1¾ to 1⅞) wide blade (Figure 6-1). The challenges increase dramatically with a 65mm or 70mm (2½" or 2¾") plane. The 45mm to 48mm size feels good in the hand, is reasonably easy to set up and maintain, is similar in blade width to Western-style smoothing planes, and serves as a good introduction to Japanese planes. With its low-friction bottom and low-effort, clean-shearing cut, it may well represent a benchmark against which to judge the performance of other planes. While it does not have an adjustable mouth or frog, the chipbreaker is easy to adjust and readjust as required for different cuts, which can be invaluable in learning this important tactic.

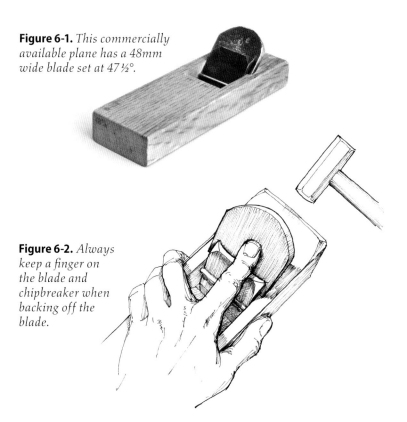

Figure 6-1. *This commercially available plane has a 48mm wide blade set at 47½°.*

Figure 6-2. *Always keep a finger on the blade and chipbreaker when backing off the blade.*

Bench Planes

1. INSPECT THE PLANE

The idea of setting aside any wooden plane for a few months before working with it is particularly important with regard to Japanese planes, as the climate is very humid in Japan, and the *dai* (block) requires considerable acclimation when moved to the (almost always) drier climate of the West. Withdraw the blade by tapping the top back edge of the dai with a very small (approximately 4 oz., or 115g) hammer or small mallet. You can turn the plane upside down when you do this to allow gravity to assist, but it is best if you grip the body with the thumb and second finger and keep the first finger on the top of the blade to keep the chipbreaker from flying out (Figure 6-2). Actually, this is the general procedure always for removing the blade and chipbreaker.

Sometimes the dai will shrink around the blade after it has been imported to our drier climate. This can be so severe that the dai cracks, or, more usually, deforms, clamping down on the blade so hard it becomes nearly impossible to remove it. Inspect for this and avoid it, if you can, when buying your plane (not usually possible on mail-order). If you end up with a plane to which this has happened, if the warp is slight and the dai is not cracked, you may be able to straighten it out by clamping it down with an equal reverse bend for several days. In the long run though, this will probably compromise getting top-notch performance out of the plane. If the dai is cracked I would send it back to the seller. The few times I have observed this malady it was in cheaper planes. In any case, remove the blade and chipbreaker and set the plane aside to let it adjust to our drier climate until it stops moving. This may be six months or more; you can set it and use it right away, but it will continue to move for a while and will need considerable and frequent readjustment until it acclimates.

2. PREPARE THE BLADE

Because the blade is wedged into the body, preparing the blade before proceeding with any of the other steps becomes particularly important. First, flatten the back as usual, but notice its hollow grind. If you have flattened other plane blades, you will especially appreciate the refinement—even more when you realize the blade steel is much harder than most blade steels. The hollow saves a lot of tedious work. The flat around the hollow grind is called the ura. The ura must be flattened across the width of the blade at the edge, and at least as far back as where the hollow grind begins.

While the blade is laid on the stone for most of its cutting length—as it is stroked the length of the stone, it must be shifted gradually across the width of the stone as you work, or it will wear the stone unevenly (and the blade)—only the last bit of blade at the edge really has to be flat.

Some craftsmen recommend tapping out the blade as part of the initial preparation, believing that this cold work helps align the crystalline structure and toughen the blade. I cannot verify that. The most common reason to do this is to speed up flattening the back, when the flat had

FLATTENING THE BACK OF THE PLANE BLADE

There are a number of techniques that can be used to flatten the back of a plane blade. Which technique to best choose in flattening a particular blade is dependent upon how much work must be done to get it flat.

No matter which technique you use, you will have to finish with your sharpening stones, and these must be flat, so start by flattening your sharpening stones. (See "Using and Maintaining Waterstones" on page 107.)

Generally, new Japanese blades will come well ground, requiring only honing on your stones to get that final flat, mirror polish. If you have a used blade that has gone out of flat, you can use a few different techniques to restore its flatness.

Before starting work on the blade, appraise the flatness of the back. Hold the blade up to a large light source, sighting along the blade so that you can catch a reflection that goes all the way across the back reflecting off the ura, or flat, that goes down the two sides and the edge. Tilt the length of the blade up and down and study the reflection. If the entire ura lights up down to the edge, you have a dead flat blade and you will only have to hone it through your usual series of stones. If, however, only a portion of the length of the blade lights up and this moves up and down the blade as you tilt it, then the blade has a curve to it, the shorter the reflection the more the curve.

In this case, you do not have to try to flatten the entire length of the blade. Technically, only that portion of the ura of a plane blade right behind the edge needs to be flattened (chisels, though, are different). It's best practice to have most, if not all of the ura in the same plane, and indeed, when flattening the back the entire blade (that is, the up to where the edge steel ends) should be laid on the stones, though the focus is on the edge. Over time the ura along the sides gets bigger from restoring the ura at

FLATTENING THE BACK OF THE PLANE BLADE *(continued)*

the edge (see "Tapping Out a Japanese Blade" on page 68), eventually threatening to over take the hollow grind. You want to postpone this happening for as long as you can, so once you have a flat behind the edge to hone to and rest the chipbreaker on, you can stop.

Finally, look at the back of the edge itself. Tilt the blade until the reflection rolls down to the edge; if you have to tilt the blade more than a little to catch a reflection there, or if you can continue tilting the blade and continue getting a reflection, you have a rounded edge. This requires removal of a lot of material and a different strategy is called for. If the edge is severely rounded this will require the removal of too much material from the back of the blade, greatly extending the ura. In this case, before starting to flatten the back, you should grind the main blade bevel back until the rounding or back bevel is eliminated. Most probably this will cause you to lose the ura at the edge and will require you to tap out the blade before beginning to flattening process.

After you have appraised the condition of the back of your blade, developed a strategy, and made sure your stones are flat, begin flattening by stroking the blade's back on your coarsest stone. Hold the blade perpendicular to the length of the stone, use the entire length of the stone, and as much of the full length of the blade as possible, back and forth, keeping at least 1" (25mm) or more of the blade on the stone at all times.

Make sure the blade stays flat on the stone—no lifting or rocking. Keep pressure on the blade right behind the edge to keep from gouging the back at the edge of the stone. After about 30 seconds to a minute, clean and look at the back of the blade. If the new flat is within about 1/32" (.8mm) of the edge at all places (and the reflection indicates it is not heavily rounded), you can probably continue using the waterstones for the whole process, moving to each individual stone as the polish pattern of each becomes continuous across and down to the entire edge.

If you have to spend more than about four or five minutes of continuous work on a waterstone, you will have to re-flatten it before continuing. Therefore, if a minute of vigorous work on the coarse stone leaves more than about 1/32" (.8mm) of edge undone, you are probably better off going instead to a coarse diamond stone to flatten the blade. If not, you can wear your waterstones out of flat, necessitating re-flattening the stones (and most probably the back of the blade as well) several times before you are done. (If you have ceramic or Arkansas stones you may be able to do the whole flattening process on either of those. Just make sure they're flat before you start and remain flat as you work as they do wear, albeit much more slowly). After the flat on the back reaches the edge, you can go back and do your normal sharpening sequence on your (flat) stones to polish the back.

If after about a minute on your coarse stone you show the new flat at 1/16" (2mm) or more away, consider measures that are more drastic (though you can continue to work away on the diamond stone if you prefer). The cheapest, fastest, and most effective way to flatten a badly out-of-flat plane-blade back is to use the Japanese method of carborundum (silicon-carbide) on an iron plate (*kanaban*). The carborundum particles grip the softer *kanaban* (though it does wear it out—eventually), and abrade the tool steel. The iron flattening plate, at Japanese tool suppliers, is about $25. An ounce of carborundum is about $3, though if you can find a lapidary supply house you can get a lifetime supply for about $5.

Figure 1. *To flatten a severely out-of-flat blade on a kanaban (iron plate), put about a small pea-size mound of carborundum in the center of the plate. Add three or four drops of water to the carborundum. In the background is a stick that can be used when holding the blade.*

FLATTENING THE BACK OF THE PLANE BLADE *(continued)*

Figure 2. *Rub the back of the blade back and forth using the whole length of the plate. Use of a stick allows you to increase the pressure on the blade at its edge while reducing finger fatigue. The blade and stick are held with the right hand, with the left hand keeping a constant downward pressure. Do not be tempted to rock the blade. The blade must remain flat on the stone at all times. If you lift the right hand even one stroke you will round the edge enough to require 10 or 15 strokes to remove the damage.*

Figure 3. *The carborundum has broken down into a paste and is rubbed until dry.*

The beauty of this method is the grit breaks down as you use it, so you can start with 60 or 90 grit, which is very coarse (for a blade in particularly bad condition), or 120 grit (if you think the blade is not too bad). Either gradually breaks down to about 6,000 grit, while increasingly refining the surface. In one step (and about three to five minutes of vigorous rubbing), you can go from a nasty old blade to a mirror-polished jewel.

To use the flattening plate, put about a small pea size amount of carborundum in the center of the plate and add 3 or 4 drops of water to it **(Figure 1).** Begin rubbing the back of the blade back and forth using the whole length of the plate. Periodically bring the excess carborundum back into the center of the plate so all the carborundum is broken down at the same rate **(Figure 2).** Stray coarse pieces of carborundum will scratch the blade, so make sure it is all used. Continue rubbing as the carborundum breaks down into a smooth paste, occasionally adding a drop or two of water if the paste gets too dry to rub. As the paste gets extremely fine, check your progress; you should see a consistent flat at the edge.

Continue rubbing until the back shows a high polish and the paste is transparently fine and rubbed dry **(Figure 3).** Then add 1 (or maybe 2) drops of water and vigorously rub until the paste is dry again. This will bring up a very high polish. Inspect the blade. Hopefully, the mirror polish of your newly flat back now extends all the way to the edge. If not, you will have to do it again, though you can probably start with 120 or 220 grit now. With the final polish, you do not have to follow up with any work on the stones; you can go right to the bevel.

Make sure to keep the carborundum separate from your stones, because it can embed itself and continue to scratch a blade for a long time. Wash the blade and everything else in separate water and rinse thoroughly.

TAPPING OUT A JAPANESE BLADE

Eventually, after many sharpenings, you will lose the *ura*, or flat, on the back of the blade at the edge **(Figure 1)**. The ura must be re-established if the blade is to be useable. Traditionally, the easiest way to do this is to tap out the blade. Not only does this save you from having to flatten the entire back but also cold-working the steel this way may add some toughness to the edge.

You will need a small anvil with a rounded corner on the top (the horn of an anvil is ok), and a small 4oz. (115g) square or octagonal hammer. Traditionally the Japanese used what looks like a section of railroad track for an anvil. This has a chamfered edge along one side for setting saws, and one or two rounded corners on one end for tapping out the blades.

Body position is important. You must be in a stable standing or sitting position where you cannot sway. The hammer arm must be locked to the side so the wrist forms an unchanging pivot point. This will allow the hammer to fall of its own weight with repeat accuracy (absolutely important!).

The corner of the hammer strikes the blade bevel on the soft backing steel, slightly closer to the edge than about midway in the width of the bevel, in a line across the width of the blade **(Figure 2)**. This will force the edge steel out a few ten-thousandths of an inch, which can be then flattened on the stones into a new ura **(Figure 3)**.

Here is the secret: the blade must be supported on the corner of the anvil exactly opposite the hammer strike. If you do not, *you can crack the edge steel.* You can tell if it is properly supported if the hammer strike results in a dull thud. If the strike causes a ringing sound then the anvil is not directly

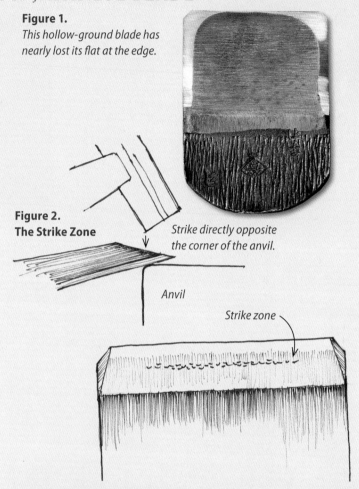

Figure 1.
This hollow-ground blade has nearly lost its flat at the edge.

Figure 2.
The Strike Zone

Strike directly opposite the corner of the anvil.

Anvil

Strike zone

Figure 3. *Swinging it from the wrist, the hammer must fall of its own weight on the bevel, slightly closer than midway to the edge. The corner of the anvil must support the blade directly under the corner of the hammer.*

TAPPING OUT A JAPANESE BLADE *(continued)*

under the hammer. Do a light trial tap to check for the sound; adjust your position until the blade no longer rings when struck but responds with a dull thud. Then strike the soft steel with slightly more than the weight of the hammer once or twice leaving a distinct mark. Work your way across the center two-thirds of the blade, doing trial taps with each re-adjustment before striking (**Figure 4**).

Once you have worked all the way cross the blade, you can flatten the back, usually on waterstones (newly flattened, of course), rather than one of the more intensive methods (see "Flattening the Back of the Plane Blade," below). If a new ura does not quickly appear when honing, go back and repeat the process (**Figure 5**).

Figure 4. *Tapping leaves a series of dimples across the soft backing-steel portion of the bevel. These do not interfere with the function of the blade and are soon honed out.*

Figure 5.
The blade with its new flat after being tapped out and honed.

been sharpened away over time. Tapping out a new blade only pushes even more blade steel out to be flattened. If you have not yet lost the edge back into the hollow grind, you are just making more work. Anyway, I suggest you get thoroughly familiar with Japanese blades before you attempt to tap one out. By the time you have sharpened the blade back into the hollow will be soon enough.

Check that the cutting edge is only as wide as the mouth opening (Figure 6-3). Grind the blade's corners back as required to narrow the edge to this width. You probably will not have to do this on a new blade, but you will as the blade wears. Otherwise, the blade will cut a shaving in the area where it is captured

Figure 6-3. Grinding Corners.

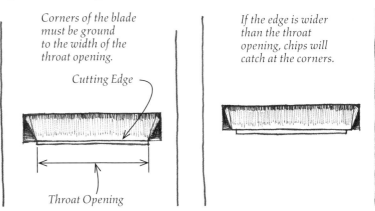

Corners of the blade must be ground to the width of the throat opening.

Cutting Edge

Throat Opening

If the edge is wider than the throat opening, chips will catch at the corners.

by the dai, which then jams with chips. Be very careful when you do this, as it is very easy to burn the blade. Try to replicate the angle it was originally ground to. Lap the burr off the back on your finish stone.

Sharpen the bevel, and then stone the outside edges off the top (hollow-ground side) of these corner grinds. Dull these slightly so they are not sharp.

3. PREPARE THE CHIP BREAKER

Begin by placing the chipbreaker on the blade in what will be its final position. Pinch the two together tightly near the cutting

edge and hold them up to the light (Figure 6-4). The blade should be flat (since you just flattened it). If there is any light coming between the two, then the chipbreaker needs to be flattened. (Do not worry if the chipbreaker does not sit flat overall on the blade at this time; that is the next step after this.) The chipbreakers on the best planes are laminated steel, similar to the blade itself. On lesser quality planes, the chipbreaker is hardened and tempered but not laminated.

Occasionally, on smaller, cheaper, usually specialty planes, I have seen some poorly formed chipbreakers that appear to be made of mild steel. You can get these to work, but they will not take much demanding service. With the better quality and laminated chipbreakers you will have to flatten them using your sharpening stones, as they are too hard to be filed. Make sure your stones are perfectly flat, and if you have to work the chipbreaker a lot, periodically re-flatten them or use a diamond stone to straighten them. The back of the chipbreaker is usually hollow-ground similar to the blade and will have the flat ura already established. Lay the ura on the stone and carefully flatten it (Figure 6-5, Figure 6-6, Figure 6-7), working through all your stones, until it has a mirror polish. The bevel edge is then stoned as well down to the fine finish stone, to a polish like the blade. Do not get overzealous and enlarge the micro bevel at the edge of the chipbreaker; you want to keep this as small as it was originally made. On a 40° plane this micro bevel is about 60° (see "Chipbreaker" on page 24).

Figure 6-4.

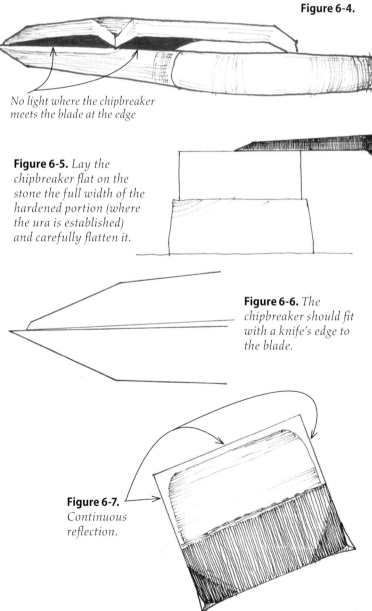

No light where the chipbreaker meets the blade at the edge

Figure 6-5. *Lay the chipbreaker flat on the stone the full width of the hardened portion (where the ura is established) and carefully flatten it.*

Figure 6-6. *The chipbreaker should fit with a knife's edge to the blade.*

Figure 6-7. *Continuous reflection.*

Once the edge of the chipbreaker is fitted, the overall fit to the blade can be completed. Set the blade down on the bench with its chipbreaker on top in its position. Hold the edge of the chipbreaker tight at its edge and alternately tap the top two corners (Figure 6-8). There will be no sound at the corners that fit tight to the blade.

If a corner is high, it will make a metallic tapping sound when tapped. Take this corner to an anvil, and, holding the chipbreaker on the edge of the anvil, aligned with the crease at the corner ear, tap the ear with a small hammer to bend it over (Figure 6-9). If you bend it too much, place the chipbreaker on top of the anvil, spanning the point of the ear and another point about equally distant into the body of the chipbreaker, and tap the bend to flatten the ear back out. Repeat this until you can hold the blade and chipbreaker tight at their cutting edges and tap both upper corners without making a sound. Later, after you have fitted the blade to the dai, you may have to do this again if the location of the cross pin is badly off, or you need more or less room under it to make the chipbreaker hold its adjustment. I've had to do this on planes where I have drilled and installed the cross pin, but I can't ever remember having to do it on a plane I bought, except perhaps one of the cheaper specialty planes with the mild steel chipbreaker.

4. FIT THE BLADE

Before beginning to fit the blade to the dai, check again the width of the blade

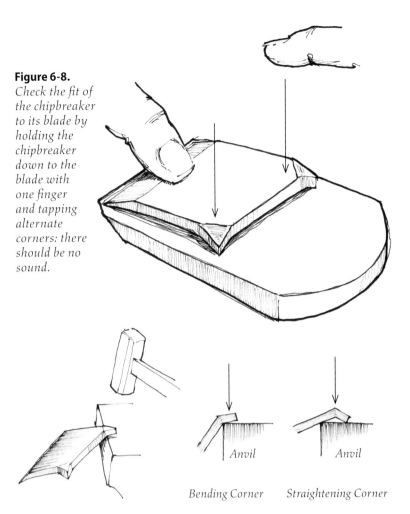

Figure 6-8.
Check the fit of the chipbreaker to its blade by holding the chipbreaker down to the blade with one finger and tapping alternate corners: there should be no sound.

Anvil   Anvil

Bending Corner   *Straightening Corner*

Figure 6-9. Proper Placement on an Anvil.

GAUGING STRAIGHTNESS
You can use feeler gauges under a straight edge to measure the amount a surface is out of flat, but it is easier to gauge the amount just by sighting under a straight edge: the human eye can see light through a gap of less than .001" (.025mm).

escapement (Figure 6-10). The opening in the dai should be perhaps ¹⁄₃₂" (.8mm) wider on either side of the blade, enough initially for the blade to slip in unimpeded by the sides. Once the blade is fitted, there must be enough space so the blade can be tapped left or right to adjust for parallel to the sole. Take a small chisel and pare a slight amount, as required, from both sides until the opening is wide enough. Also, check that the opening is wide enough for the chipbreaker. If it is not, then the cross pin must be driven back out, and the chip well pared slightly wider to accommodate it.

Once the width of the blade opening has been checked and the blade and chipbreaker prepared, final fitting of the blade can begin. The blade is fit independently of

Figure 6-10: Bed the Blade Properly

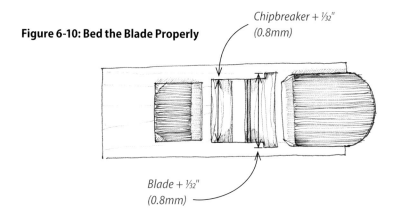

*Chipbreaker + ⅟₃₂"
(0.8mm)*

*Blade + ⅟₃₂"
(0.8mm)*

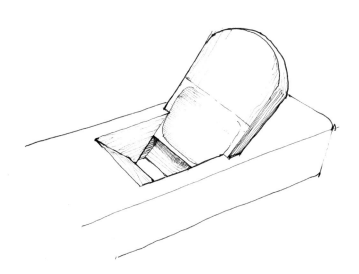

Figure 6-11. *When first fitting the blade, put the blade into the plane, pushing it in by hand as far as you can. The further in you can push it, the less material you will have to remove to fit it.*

the chipbreaker, and does not require any wedging action from it. The chipbreaker, in fact should be a gentle fit, no tighter than is required to maintain its setting. Set the chipbreaker aside, and put the blade into the plane, pushing it in by hand as far as you can (Figure 6-11). When the blade is finally fit, you should be able to push it in to within about ⅛" (3mm) of its final position. (This depends some on the nature of the piece of wood used for the dai: you should be able to push it in by hand a little more if the block is more resistant, a little less if it has some give. In other words, if the dai is very hard it will have less give and the blade must be fitted closer to its working position so that you don't have to drive it into position with heavy hammer blows and stress the block.) Chances are the blade will go in far short of its final position.

The underside of the blade is concave across its width (Figure 6-12). This means the blade bed is convex, and a close look at the area confirms it (Figure 6-13). Often the bed is a little too convex. You want to fit this curve to the blade along its entire captured length so the blade makes solid contact with the bed at all points, and especially at the outside edges at the side groove. The upper edges of the side groove are not worked, because they are the reference surfaces that position the blade. Withdraw the blade by tapping the top back edge of the dai with a very small hammer or mallet while holding the blade with two fingers and the dai with the rest of the hand. Coat the back of the blade with graphite (by rubbing it with a pencil), ink, or (strangely enough) Vaseline (how I was shown). Push the blade in and tap it in a little deeper with three or four taps of the hammer. Then tap the back of the dai again and remove the blade. The pencil (ink, Vaseline) will have marked the high spots on the blade bed of the dai. With a freshly sharpened chisel, carefully pare away the stains left by the marking (Figure 6-14), only enough to remove the mark. Reinsert the blade as before and remove. Pare again.

Continue until the blade goes to within hammer-tapping distance of a working position. You will have to recoat the back of the blade periodically. Do not get impatient and pare away any more than the finest shaving, slightly more than dust. This whole procedure usually takes at least five passes—maybe as many as 30—but not usually that many. The blade should fit tightly in its escapement, particularly at its outer edges, where it is captured. Do not neglect to coat the back of the blade all the way to its outer edges, and to carefully check the corresponding part of the blade bed when fitting the blade, as it hard to see into the slot and thus easy to neglect.

If you pare away too much and the blade slides in too far, finish fitting the blade making sure it is solidly bedded, even though it may protrude too far. Then you can glue a piece of paper to the blade bed to shim the blade tighter. Try a piece of onionskin paper first because it does not take much to tighten up the fit of the blade; often a piece of 20-lb.

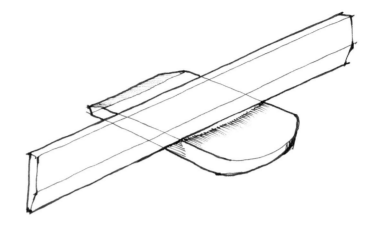

Figure 6-12 *The underside of a traditional Japanese blade is not flat, but concave across its width.*

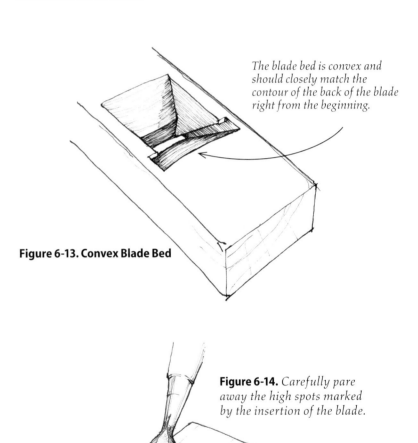

The blade bed is convex and should closely match the contour of the back of the blade right from the beginning.

Figure 6-13. Convex Blade Bed

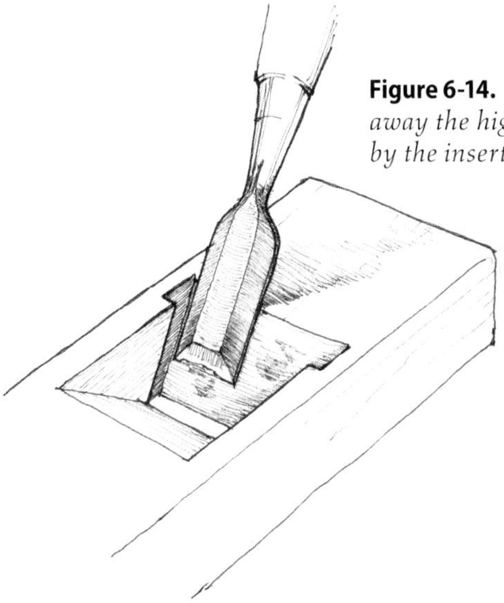

Figure 6-14. *Carefully pare away the high spots marked by the insertion of the blade.*

Figure 6-15 *After several years, the self-wedging blade can become too loose to hold its adjustment. Remedy the problem by gluing a piece of paper to the bed. Here, a piece of very lightweight tracing paper was sufficient to correct the fit.*

Figure 6-16. *When paring the blade slot with a chisel, also work in through the mouth.*

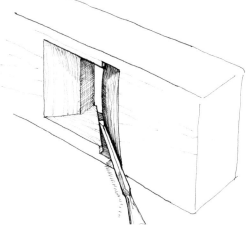

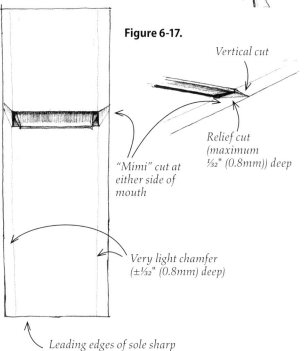

Figure 6-17.

Vertical cut

Relief cut (maximum ¹⁄₃₂" (0.8mm)) deep

"Mimi" cut at either side of mouth

Very light chamfer (±¹⁄₃₂" (0.8mm) deep)

Leading edges of sole sharp

typing paper will be too much (Figure 6-15). If it is very loose, a piece of brown craft paper (like from a paper bag) can be used. Eventually, you will probably have to shim the blade because it also loosens with time and use.

Once the blade is fitted, tap the blade to its working position and check again that it has enough room on either side for lateral adjustment. If not, remove the blade and pare away the sides of the blade slot as required (Figure 6-16). Reinstall the blade and tap the chipbreaker into working position. Do not force it; if it is too tight, flatten the ears out a bit as described earlier. If it is too loose, bend the ears over a bit. Make sure the chipbreaker still sits flat on the blade by tapping the ears as described.

5. CONFIGURE THE SOLE

Install the blade and chipbreaker and tap them to within about ¹⁄₁₆" (2mm) of the bottom, maybe a little closer, but make sure the blade is back from the bottom (you will be removing material from the bottom, so pay attention) and the chipbreaker is set within working distance of the blade edge. Now the sole of the plane can be prepared.

Before you begin conditioning the sole, you can plane a slight chamfer of just a few degrees down both sides of the plane's sole, just to the width of the blade opening (Figure 6-17). I actually like to chamfer the edges all the way to the cutting edge. It reduces the area of the sole, which must be conditioned, to the width of the blade. This is not so much a laborsaving device, but one that helps eliminate trouble spots later.

Often the plane's sole will contact the work in an area outside the blade path. Some of these areas are easy to miss when checking the sole for flatness, especially at either side of the blade, and will prevent the plane from cutting because they are high and contact the work, or will leave an annoying burnished spot making the texture of the finished surface inconsistent. On a truing plane, though, you may not want to have a chamfer quite that wide because you may want as much reference area as possible contacting the work in order to have the flattest resulting surface.

Besides the chamfer, you should also make a couple of relief cuts (*mimi*) on either side of the blade to allow chips, which tend to get caught at the outside edges of the blade where the dai wedges the blade, to escape, and to aid in conditioning the sole.

Choose the configuration of the bottom by the type of plane you have or function you wish it to perform: roughing, truing, or smoothing or variations of these (Figure 6-18). Put a straightedge on the bottom and first check that the area directly in front of the mouth is flat across the width of the plane, not curved from wood movement or wear (Figure 6-19). Flatten this if necessary. Then check the length for contact points at both sides and the center. Check across the width for straight, and check all the contact spots across the width for parallel by using winding sticks. Also, check diagonally (Figure 6-20). All of these points are checked by holding the straightedge and plane up to the light (Figure 6-21). If the sole is badly out of flat, you may have to use another plane, finely set, which you know is accurate, to initially level the bottom. (I have never had

WHAT REALLY HAPPENS

If you examined what happens when a plane cuts, it might appear the area behind the blade should be exactly in line with the blade edge and project more than the two areas in front—much like how the outfeed table of a power jointer is set up—nearly even with the cutters.

In practice, however, it is often helpful to slightly relieve the third working surface, not only from the blade edge, but often from the other two leading surfaces as well. This is because as the blade edge wears, it withdraws—gets shorter (see "**How an Edge Dulls**" on page 27) and a plane bottom that was fixed even with the sharpened edge would soon hold the worn edge off the work.

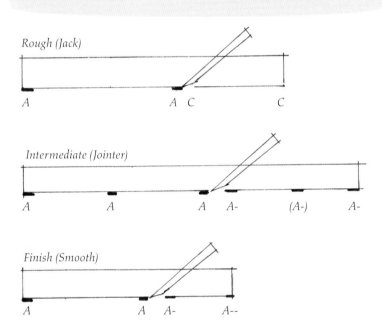

Figure 6-18. Schematic of Contact Areas of the Sole of Japanese-Style Planes. *Contact areas extend the full width of the plane, are parallel, and are on a line with one another except where they have been relieved slightly as suggested in the illustration. Areas between contact areas are relieved only a few thousandths of an inch. A to C <1/64"; A to A-: 1 or 2 passes with a card scraper; A to A--: 2 to 4.*

to use a power jointer to level the bottom.) A scraper plane with a longish sole and a straight blade (not the Stanley #80) can be also used.

I know this goes counter to most of what you will read, but the sole of a wood plane, and especially a Japanese plane, is *never* sanded. There are good reasons for it. Mainly, sanding embeds grit into the bottom of the plane and

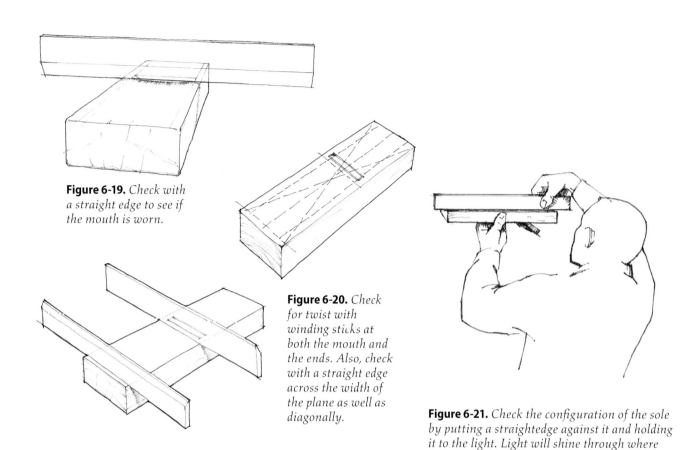

Figure 6-19. *Check with a straight edge to see if the mouth is worn.*

Figure 6-20. *Check for twist with winding sticks at both the mouth and the ends. Also, check with a straight edge across the width of the plane as well as diagonally.*

Figure 6-21. *Check the configuration of the sole by putting a straightedge against it and holding it to the light. Light will shine through where the straight edge does not contact the sole.*

THE OILER

For all styles of planes and planing, it is helpful to have a large oiler sitting on the bench. Drag the sole of the plane over it (backward) periodically while working, to keep the sole of the plane—and the blade edge as well—lubricated while working. This allows planing rhythm to be virtually uninterrupted.

The oiler should be around 3" (76mm) in diameter: a lidded canister, a drilled out block of wood, or, traditionally, a large bamboo knuckle. Rip rags to about 3" or 4" (76mm or 102mm) wide. It will take most or all of a bed sheet. Wrap the rags continuously in a coil until you reach the desired diameter—usually slightly larger than the hole it is to go into. Wrap the end to be inserted with heavy plastic such as a plastic drop cloth or Visqueen, and work the whole roll into the hole. About ½" (13mm) or more of the cloth should protrude from the container; cut the plastic off even with the container. Saturate the cloth with camellia oil (available at Japanese tools suppliers), which provides light, contaminate-free lubrication.

Two oilers, both made from a section of bamboo. *The larger one is about 3" (76mm) in diameter and sits on the bench when used. Take the plane to the oiler and stroke its sole over it during planing as part of the rhythm of work. The smaller one is about 1½" (38mm) in diameter and is picked up to be used.*

WINDING STICKS

Winding sticks can be any two sticks that are rectangular in section and long enough to lie across the work you are checking. The sticks need to be straight and have the two parallel edges. For checking timber, the sticks do not have to be of great refinement: you can literally grab two sticks out of the scrap pile—they don't even have to be the same width—as long as they are straight and parallel. The longer they are, the greater the accuracy in checking for parallel, as the greater length exaggerates the distortion.

Figure 1. *A matched set of wood winding sticks.*

If you want a tool of greater sophistication, you can buy wood and metal ones, or you can make you own. When making your own, the principal is simple enough. Pin two pieces of wood together so they can be separated, plane both edges straight, pull them apart, and check them by holding the edges together up to the light. Any error in straightness doubles. If light shines between the edges at any point, put them back together and plane them until no light is visible when they are held against one another. If the pieces are used in the same orientation as when they are pinned together (make a habit of doing this), it will make no difference, even if a taper has been planed along their length, because the pieces will still be parallel to one another **(Figure 1)**.

it is released gradually during use of the plane, dulling the blade for some time to come. (For the same reason, you should never plane a surface that has been previously sanded, as the grit left in the surface will also rapidly dull a plane blade.) Anyway, sanding is too slow and tedious if any amount has to be taken off, and will distort the bottom. The bottom needs to be finessed to within a few thousandths of an inch and sandpaper can't do that.

Instead the sole is configured using the Japanese scraper, made for this purpose (Figure 6-22). It is the tool of choice for shaping the sole of the plane. They come in different sizes for different size planes, and craftsmen will make different sizes, often from a miscellaneous plane blade they have around, for specific tasks. Except for the widest ones, which are for general leveling, Japanese scrapers are used to attack

specific high spots, first lowering the non-contact areas below the contact areas, and then bringing the contact areas into line as required by the desired bottom configuration. The Japanese scraper plane is used mostly across the grain; sometimes a bit diagonally to even things up if required. Because it is scraping across the grain, I find the cut it makes can be a bit rough. Sometimes, after the bottom geometry has been established, I go over areas I think need attention with a card scraper.

Figure 6-22. *A typical Japanese scraper plane used to condition the sole of Japanese planes. The blade is 45mm wide, mounted at 90°. The sides have been heavily chamfered off nearly to the edge of the blade to increase visibility right at the edge of the area being conditioned.*

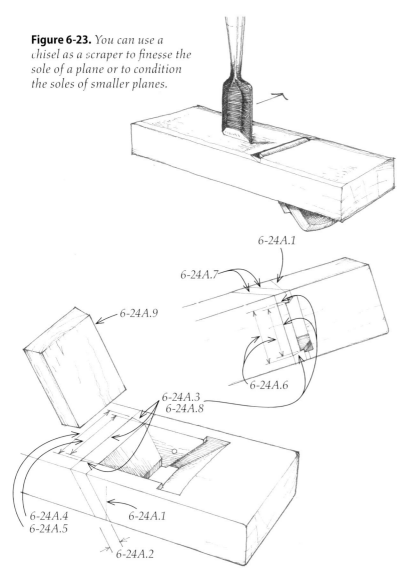

Figure 6-23. *You can use a chisel as a scraper to finesse the sole of a plane or to condition the soles of smaller planes.*

6-24A.1

6-24A.7

6-24A.9

6-24A.6

6-24A.3
6-24A.8

6-24A.4
6-24A.5

6-24A.1

6-24A.2

Figure 6-24A. Fitting a Sliding Dovetail Key, or Kuchi-ire, to Close a Mouth Worn Open. *A kuchi-ire is a dovetailed piece set into a plane as a repair to close the mouth. Because end grain bears on the work, this is a durable (and re-adjustable) repair.*

- *6-24A.1. Mark position of blade edge around the block.*
- *6-24A.2. Determine thickness of replacement piece; transfer lines to sides of dai (see Figure 6-24B).*
- *6-24A.3. Mark out dovetail as shown.*
- *6-24A.4. Equal to chipwell opening.*
- *6-24A.5. Equal to chipwell opening plus ⅟₁₆" (2mm).*
- *6-24A.6. Equal to the top.*
- *6-24A.7. Transfer layout lines from the top to the bottom.*
- *6-24A.8. Cut the dovetail line to the outside of the line on the top and to in inside of the line on the bottom, thus giving a slight taper to the opening.*
- *6-24A.9. Cut the replacement piece to the full width of the dovetailed mortise and then plane a slight taper into it by taking partial-length shavings with a plane to induce a taper. Test the fit one shaving at a time until it can be tapped (tap is the operative word here!) into place.*

If you don't have a Japanese scraper plane, you can use a chisel held vertically as a scraper, and use a card scraper to finish if you want (Figure 6-23).

Every day you use your planes, you should check their sole configuration before starting work, like warming up before doing exercise, and touch them up as required. This is especially true of fine finish planes, which take a very fine cut. In fact, if they are not giving the service you expect, you may have to check and tune them during the day as you work with them. Generally though, once the plane has acclimated, and if your shop does not go through big temperature and humidity swings, you will find the planes rather stable, and except perhaps for achieving the very demanding, smoothing cut, will not require that much maintenance. Remember at the end of every day, and when you are not using them, to loosen the blade, just to where they will not fall out when you pick them up.

6. ADJUST THE MOUTH

Most often on a new manufactured plane I do not do any fitting of a *kuchi-ire* (sole plate) (Figures 6-24A to 6-24F), relying instead largely on the quality of the blade and the effectiveness of the chipbreaker. I find the mouth opening on the new planes is usually accurately formed, tight, and does not otherwise need any attention. As to used planes, unfortunately, not many in serviceable condition reach our shores. I have seen many, though, that are a day short of being wore out, with badly worn *kuchi-ire* (sole plate) repairs that are themselves old, with the dais worn down to a third of their original thickness and blades with ¼" (6mm) or less of serviceable edge steel left. Sadly, these cannot be reconditioned and put back into service, but they look as if they have served their original masters well.

7. ATTEND TO THE DETAILS OF THE BODY AND SOLE

Now you can finish detailing the dai. It is good practice to make sure the sides of the dai are square to the sole. It is mandatory if the plane is to be used on its side to joint boards. If you did not add the slight chamfers at the edges of the sole and the relief cuts when first configuring the sole, as described in that section, you can do that now if you wish. The leading edges of the bottom are left sharp. This is to prevent errant shavings from sliding under the plane and causing it to ride up. The front edge under the blade bed can be squared off to help prevent chipping there

Generally, outside edges are gently rounded to be easy on the hand. The top edge behind the blade is rounded more, as are the corners of that edge, to reduce damage from the adjusting hammer (Figure 6-25).

A final optional step is to saturate the dai with camellia oil. The few times I have done this, I am not sure I have been happy with the results. A full description of the process can be found in "Making a Japanese-Style Plane" on page 122.

Tap the blade and chipbreaker down to a working position, make a light cut, and take a trial shaving. Because you know the blade is sharp, if it will not cut, the sole is not flat. Back the blade off just enough to clear

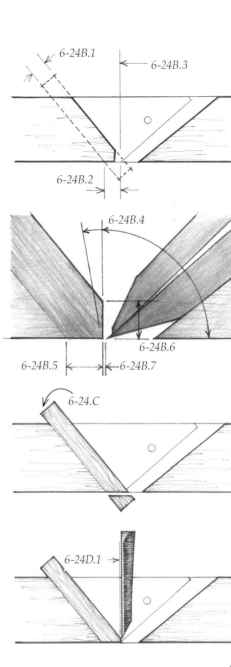

Figure 6-24B. *Determining the thickness of the kuchi-ire*

- *6-24B.1. Piece must be thick enough so that there is a minimum of ⅛" left at the mouth (though a little more is better).*
- *6-24B.2. Min. ⅛"*
- *6-24B.3. Blade line*
- *6-24B.4. 90°-100°*
- *6-24B.5. ⅛"-¼"*
- *6-24B.6. + 3⁄16"*
- *6-24B.7. Tiny*

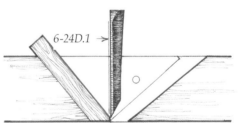

Figure 6-24C. *Fit the piece, tap it in with some paste glue and cut the bottom flush.*

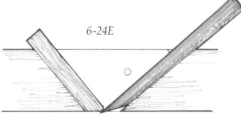

Figure 6-24D. *Trim the piece just short of the blade line, at 90°.*

- *6-24D.1. Blade line*

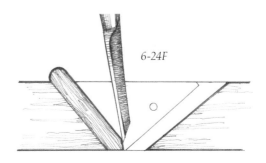

Figure 6-24E. *Insert the blade and tap it home to trim the piece right at the blade line.*

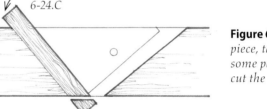

Figure 6-24F. *Trim the piece to the blade line from the top at more or less 100°. Trial fit the blade to check the size of the mouth opening. Pare as required to get the mouth opening you want.*

ADJUSTING A JAPANESE PLANE

Put the blade into the plane first, pushing it in and then tapping it a few times to make it fit snuggly, and then insert the chipbreaker. Tap the chipbreaker down gently to make it snug, but be careful you do not push it down further than the blade edge. Grab the plane with your non-hammer hand. Keep your first or second finger on the blade/chipbreaker to keep them from falling out and turn the plane over. Sighting down the sole, with your elbow locked to your side for stability, tap the blade until you can just see it protrude **(Figure 1).**

Turn the plane back over, and sighting from the top adjust the chipbreaker down until it is in close proximity to the edge (but not its final position).

Turn the plane over again, and sighting down the bottom, adjust the blade to its final position. Adjust the blade laterally by tapping one side of the blade or the other.

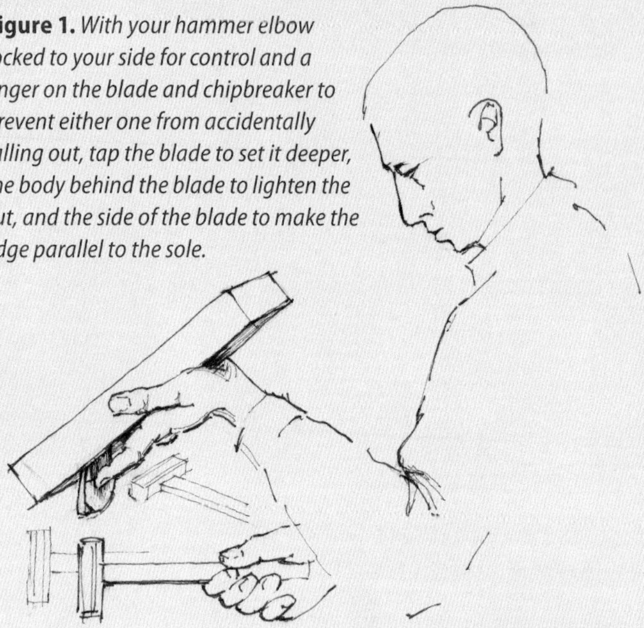

Turn the plane over again and tap the chipbreaker to its final position, adjusting it parallel to the blade edge by tapping down one corner or the other. Besides tapping the sides of the blade for lateral adjustment, you can fine-tune the blade position by tapping the top of the blade (as opposed to the side) on one corner or the other. Likewise, you tap the back corners of the dai on one side or the other to gently back that side of the blade off.

To withdraw the blade, you can turn it over so gravity assists—though it is not necessary and I often do this without turning it over. With a finger or two of one hand (probably the left) on the blade/chipbreaker, tap the back top edge of the dai with the hammer/mallet until the blade loosens.

Figure 1. *With your hammer elbow locked to your side for control and a finger on the blade and chipbreaker to prevent either one from accidentally falling out, tap the blade to set it deeper, the body behind the blade to lighten the cut, and the side of the blade to make the edge parallel to the sole.*

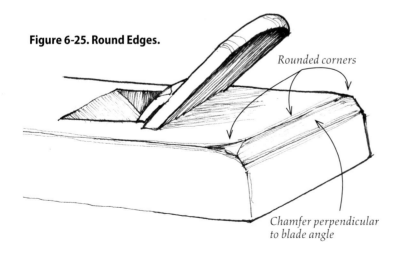

Figure 6-25. Round Edges.

Rounded corners

Chamfer perpendicular to blade angle

the bottom, and check for flat. It is easy to misread the straightedges or to miss an area. Touch up the bottom, and try a cut again. The degree of flatness will determine how fine a cut you can make. Continue this process until the plane makes the cut you want.

Figure 6-26. *A typical Japanese shouldered-blade rabbet plane.*

Setting Up Rabbet Planes

The same procedures, in the same order, are followed when setting up the rabbet plane as when setting up a bench plane. Some things, however, are done a little differently, as follows.

SETTING UP THE SHOULDERED-BLADE RABBET PLANE

1. Inspect the plane

Large portions of a rabbet-plane's body are often cut away to provide chip clearance or to allow the blade to do its job. Check for cracks at all narrowed portions of the plane, especially if there is pressure associated with them (such as from blade wedging action). Many cracks in wood planes can be repaired if not too deep or not in an area of pressure (Figure 6-27). Rabbet planes will often suffer from the same malady as the bench planes with a blade that has had the wood body shrink around it tight. Once the blade is removed, though, the escapement for the blade can be widened.

The most important thing to know about a rabbet plane is that the blade must be able to protrude on its cutting side(s) about 1⁄64" (.4mm) or maybe a little less. This seems counter-intuitive, but is proven with experience: unless the blade protrudes slightly, the plane will step away from the cut line as the cut deepens, resulting in an out-of-square shoulder and a generally narrower rabbet. I think this happens because when wood is cut there is a slight bit of compression and then springback. Though this is virtually negligible on a single cut, with repeated cuts it's additive. This is particularly true as the side of the blade is

Figure 6-27. Repairing a crack. *First, the crack in the sole behind the blade will be cleaned by cutting into it with a thin-kerf saw blade (left or top). The tapered sliver sitting on the vise will be glued in (right or bottom). Notice how the previous owner opened up the chipwell with a gouge. You are now ready to prepare the sole.*

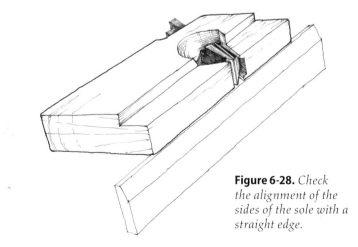

Figure 6-28. *Check the alignment of the sides of the sole with a straight edge.*

not actually cutting the fibers, but tearing them away.

Check when you first get the plane, that the blade is slightly wider than the plane body. (This check is not necessary on a one-sided rabbet plane, obviously. Just make sure the blade can be positioned proud of the side and the blade parallel to the sole.)

If for some reason the blade exceeds ¹⁄₆₄" (.4mm) on both cutting sides (an old wood-body plane can have shrunk or been worn away by at least that much), then the blade can be carefully ground narrower, or the sole portion can be replaced if it is warped (a distinct possibility) and made the same width as the blade.

Sight along the sole or use a straight edge (Figure 6-28). Oftentimes the front and back portions of the sole will have twisted out of line; this is especially true of an old plane. On a new plane, there should be little of this, because if the sole is straightened you will be removing material usually in the area of the blade, thus reducing the plane's width. The blade will then protrude too far, necessitating grinding the blade. I would consider returning such a new plane. On an old plane, this is quite common, almost to be expected. This area can be sawn off if bad enough and replaced, or the blade lightly ground narrower. Theoretically, you paid less for this plane.

2. Prepare the blade

After inspecting your plane—and establishing that the blade width is ok—begin setting it up by sharpening the blade. Using the same procedures described for preparing the blade of a smoothing plane on page 65, flatten the back first. The bevel must then be sharpened straight across, no curvature, and must be square enough to its length so it can be made parallel to the sole within the plane's range of adjustment (usually not very much) (Figures 6-29, 6-30).

3. Prepare and fit the chipbreaker (if there is one)

Fitting a chipbreaker is pretty much the same as with the bench plane. You can refer to the general procedures "Prepare the Chipbreaker" on page 70.

4. Bed the blade properly

Inspect the blade bed for flaws. This is done similarly to the bench planes, using graphite, ink, or Vaseline to mark the high spots and paring these away until the blade seats solidly (Figure 6-31). Since the blade is not captured by tapered escapements, but is held in place by the chipbreaker, you don't want to pare anymore than what will give you solid bearing as removing wood here loosens the fit. Fortunately the blade is so massive it is somewhat forgiving of its fit.

Insert the chipbreaker up through the mouth pretty much as far as it will go, and then insert the blade up also through the mouth carefully slipping it past the chipbreaker, trying not to nick it. Then, holding the blade roughly in position with one hand, slide the chipbreaker down into its position. You should have to tap the

Figure 6-29.

Restoration of a Japanese-style rabbet plane: blade and chipbreaker before (Figure 6-29) and after (Figure 6-30). When I got the plane the blades were nearly rusted together, and firmly stuck in the plane. However, the blade and chipbreaker were not pitted and cleaned up nicely.

Figure 6-30.

chipbreaker into its final position on the positioned blade—with light taps. If the chipbreaker only begrudgingly moves into final position with increasingly heavy hammer taps, it's too tight. Pare a little (very little!) away from the wood the chipbreaker bears on. If the chipbreaker can be pushed beyond the blade edge by hand, then it is too loose. Shim the wood that the chipbreaker bears against with a single piece of paper. If still too lose, try another sheet of paper.

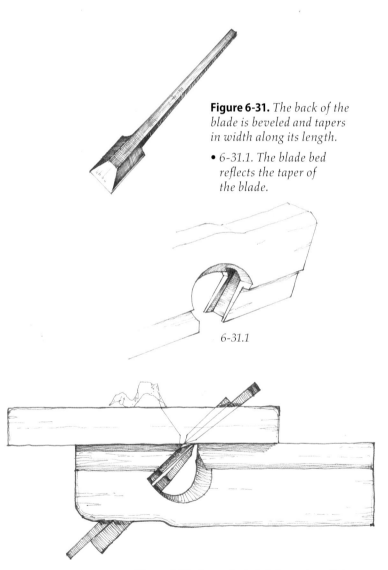

Figure 6-31. *The back of the blade is beveled and tapers in width along its length.*

• *6-31.1. The blade bed reflects the taper of the blade.*

6-31.1

Figure 6-32. *It can be helpful to take a light plane stroke off the sole behind the blade as this area is under a lot of pressure and may flex down and hold the blade off the work, preventing it from cutting.*

5. Configure the sole

In addition to flattening the sole, make sure both sides are straight (they tend to get pushed out of line around the blade) as well as square to the sole. Remember, when flattening the sole to put the blade in place at full operating pressure, about ¹⁄₁₆" (2mm) shy of the sole. On this style of rabbet plane open on both sides, the blade bed is supported only by the bulk of wood behind it and so pushes the sole down behind the blade a greater amount than many other planes. After planing the sole flat with a jointer plane, I remove a little extra from the area behind the blade with a scraper (± .01", or .25mm) to compensate for the extra flex. Alternatively, after planing the sole flat, you can place your jointer's blade at the mouth of the rabbet plane and take one or two light strokes off the area behind the blade to lower it (Figure 6-32).

Sometimes, the traditional wood rabbet plane is badly twisted with the area in front and behind the blade badly misaligned. Straightening this up with a plane might remove too much wood. You can remedy this by cutting a portion of the sole off and re-gluing a continuous piece back on (Figures 6-35A to 6-35D). After the glue has set, the blade bed and mouth opening can be cut back in. This also gives you the chance to cut a new, tighter mouth opening.

6. Adjust the mouth

If you have an old plane and the mouth has worn large, you can repair it as described above for fixing a twisted sole, if the sole has a twist; or you can inlay a patch 1" or 2" (25mm or 51mm) long and ¼" (6mm) thick to close the gap. Or you can live with it: you'll find that the chipbreaker by itself is pretty good at reducing tearout.

7. Attend to the details of the body and sole

All rabbet planes have a strong tendency to jam with chips. The solution can be as simple as frequently pushing the shaving out the exit hole—sometimes as often as every stroke of the plane. This can become a little annoying, but if you forget to do it, the consequence is worse: the shavings become tightly jammed, and clearing them entails a prolonged struggle. And it becomes even more frustrating when you have to do this repeatedly.

If your plane does this, you can open the chip spillway. This is best accomplished by paring the opening a little more on one side to exaggerate the funnel shape so that the shaving has a tendency to spiral out the side when it hits the top of the chip opening, rather than getting captured and bunching up. Figure 6-34 shows the gouge marks left from where the previous owner opened this up. You can use a gouge for the initial opening, followed by a small half-round rasp and files. You may not be able to actually get it to spiral out the side, but at least it will make the plane easier to clean out. Just do not remove too much wood and weaken the plane.

The rest of the procedures are similar to the bench planes.

Figure 6-33. *Preparing the sole of a wood rabbet plane. Besides the split that had to be repaired (See Figure 6-27, page 82), this plane had a broken nail embedded in its sole that had to be set below the surface before it could be planed.*

Figure 6-34. The finished plane. *It hurt me to remove some of the beautiful patina that the plane had acquired, but now it works beautifully.*

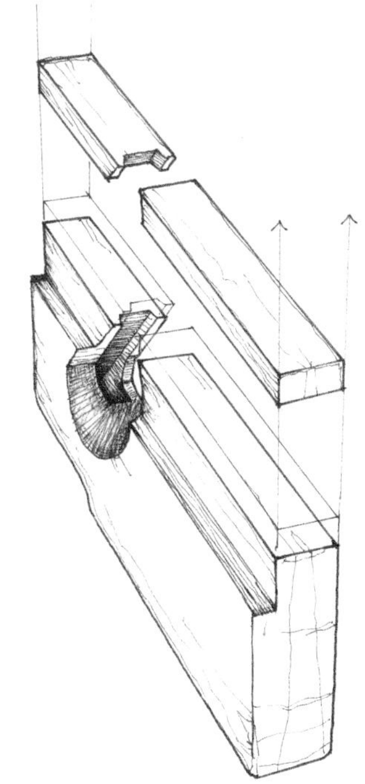

Figure 6-35A. *To straighten a twisted sole, you can cut a portion of it off, usually just to the depth of the bevel of the blade (so you don't have to re-bed the blade), and glue a continuous pice back on. When the glue is dry you can cut the mouth opening tight to the blade and finish cutting the opening by cutting the waste away at the blade seat. Come back and finish paring the blade seat to match the existing configuration.*

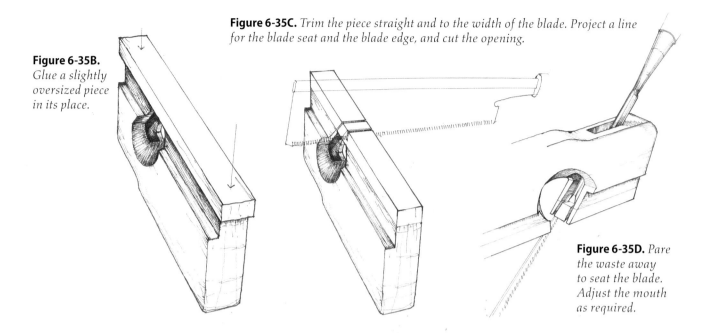

Figure 6-35B. *Glue a slightly oversized piece in its place.*

Figure 6-35C. *Trim the piece straight and to the width of the blade. Project a line for the blade seat and the blade edge, and cut the opening.*

Figure 6-35D. *Pare the waste away to seat the blade. Adjust the mouth as required.*

SKEW-BLADE RABBET PLANE

Setting up the skew-blade rabbet plane involves some additional steps. First, prepare the blade and chipbreaker, and fit the blade to its bed. This is done using the same procedures as with the bench plane. Check that the blade slot that captures the blade allows enough lateral adjustment so the blade can be adjusted both parallel to the sole as well as about ¹⁄₆₄" (.4mm) proud of the side. If not, carefully pare the side of the slot with a narrow chisel to increase lateral adjustability. Try to do most of the paring on the side with the most material so as to not weaken the cutting side of the plane.

With a skew-blade rabbet plane, you will have to establish (or maintain) the correct angle of the blade to accomplish the same parallel relation to the sole. You will not be able to check it with a square, so, if you have lost the correct angle, it may take some putting it in and out of the plane to get it right. Once you get it right you might want to make a template.

All rabbet planes have an inherent problem with chip clearance, and this plane is no exception. Its chip-clearance problem happens right at the point of the blade. This hole is often cut square; it has to be flared on the inside (chip well) side so the chips can move on into the chip well (or the outside) and out

Figure 6-36. *A Japanese skew-blade rabbet plane. These come left and right.*

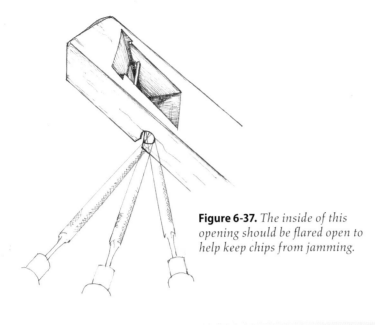

Figure 6-37. *The inside of this opening should be flared open to help keep chips from jamming.*

Figure 6-38. *A Japanese skew-blade moving fillister plane.*

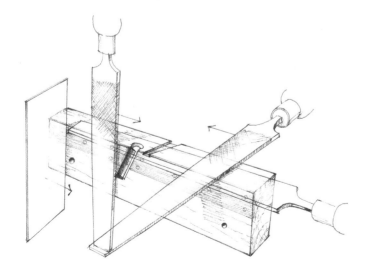

Figure 6-39. *Files and cabinet scrapers can be used to true and condition the sole and side of a fillister plane with a brass sole.*

(Figure 6-37). Using a small round file, flare the inside of the hole on the side of the plane above the point—just a little. You do not want to weaken the plane. Proceed a little at a time, alternately using the plane and flaring the hole, until it stops jamming.

True up the sole, similar to the method used for bench planes, and then square the side. You can use another finely set plane for this; be careful of the crosspin as it is on this side. It usually is slightly recessed—though not much—to allow for truing the side. I've relieved the part of the sole opposite the cutting side with a shallow, wide chamfer to reduce maintenance, but I'm having second thoughts about this. Truing the entire sole instead may give the plane better reference when planing areas wider than the blade.

SKEW-BLADE MOVING FILLISTER PLANE

This plane will be the skew blade rabbet plane with the addition of a fence and usually a scoring blade. Both planes are set up the same way, so you can set up the blade, chipbreaker, and mouth opening as described before.

Most often this plane will have a brass wear plate the length of the sole and the width of the cut. This can be configured using files and scrapers (wood scrapers can be used on the soft brass). As with all planes, remember to install the blade and chipbreaker up to tension (but retracted from the opening) when configuring the sole. A good large file can be used to shoot the side square (Figure 6-39).

The scoring blade should be set almost imperceptibly proud of the side of the plane. This is to counteract the slight springback at the cut line and thus avoid the cut stepping out as it proceeds. This cutter is fit into a tapering dovetail, so paring or shimming at the back to get alignment at the side will also affect how far the blade descends. It only needs to be set slightly deeper than the thickest shaving you intend to make. Shim with very thin paper if required (Figure 6-40).

Figure 6-40. Fitting the Scoring Blade

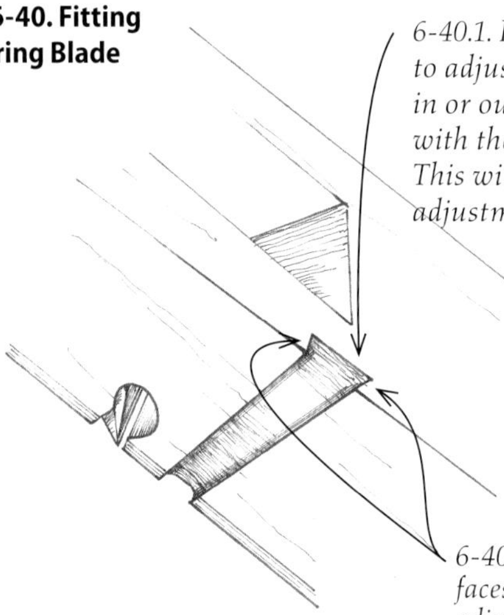

6-40.1. Pare or shim this face to adjust the scoring blade in or out to make it flush with the side of the plane. This will change its depth adjustment.

6-40.2. Pare or shim these faces to change the depth adjustment.

Figure 6-41. *One style of Japanese side rabbet plane: a single blade side rabbet.*

When using the plane, the blade should be set anywhere from flush to a very slight projection beyond the scroing blade—it depends on the plane and the wood. If the wood tears up beyond the rabbet, then the blade is set too far beyond the side of the scoring blade. If the plane steps out in the cut, the blade is set too far in. If the blade cannot be reset to a satisfactory position, the scoring blade may have to be shimmed slightly proud of the side of the plane (a paper thickness or less).

The fence must be straight, square to the sole, able to be made parallel to the side of the plane, and able to be securely fixed. The fence should not flex under normal use. Also verify and correct if necessary, that the nuts that secure the fence clear the work when tightened.

Setting Up Side-rabbet Planes

There are two basic types of side rabbet planes: single blade, and those with a chipbreaker. The basic techniques for setting up these planes are the same as for the others, but the geometry can be impressive, if not a bit confounding.

SINGLE-BLADE SIDE-RABBET PLANES

I don't know who thought this one up, but this is about as simple—and as difficult—as can be. A single blade wedged into a slot in the side of a block of wood. Because this is in an open slot rather than a mortise, this plane is prone to warping. I have an antique and it's warped in two directions, obviously from the pressure of the blade. I straightened out the cutting face, but it flexes very slightly when the blade is adjusted to cut. This is not that big a problem as it doesn't keep the plane from cutting, but if you're not paying attention the side of the rabbet you're trimming could take on the same curve. Despite all this, I like the plane: it cuts well, is easier to adjust than its Western counterparts, and is comfortable to use. I angled the bottom of the plane to match the angle of my (German) dovetail plane, so I can trim the side of tapered dovetail slots to fit. It will, of course, also trim the side of square rabbets.

As with all the Japanese planes, prepare the blade first: flatten the back and sharpen the bevel. The blade is tapered in its length being thicker at the top; and in its width, being thicker at the captured edge side, thus dovetailing it into the body and helping resist rotation in use (Figure 6-42).

Use the same technique of coating the blade and inserting it to mark the high spots. Pare these gently away until the blade can be tapped to working position. This takes a very thin chisel and it is difficult to see into the slots. Also make sure the slot is deep enough to allow lateral adjustment. Sometimes you may have to tap the side of the blade (above the edge!) with a wooden mallet to adjust its depth of cut. If the blade is too loose, or won't hold its adjustment, shim with very thin paper. In use the tip of the blade should not extend below the bottom of the plane (Figure 6-43).

DOUBLE-BLADE SIDE-RABBET PLANES

A marvelous example of geometric visualization, this plane is a nice solution to the problem of trimming the sides of rabbets, and is capable of giving a finished surface with its use of a chipbreaker.

The blade is wedge shape, thicker at the top and tapering in thickness toward the blade though it doesn't fit into matching escapements like its bench plane cousins. Instead, the chipbreaker wedges the blade tight. It must do

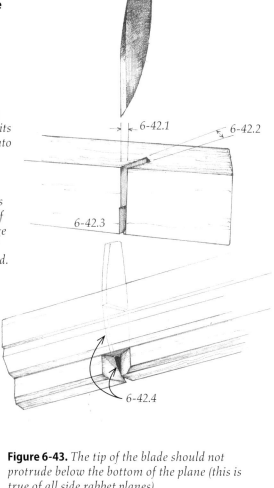

Figure 6-42. The Japanese single blade side rabbet plane. *The blade is tapered along its length.*

- *6-42.1 The blade is tapered along its length.*
- *6-42.2. The blade is also tapered across its width, dovetailed into the body.*
- *6-42.3. Blade opening.*
- *6-42.4. Blade seat is fitted to the curve of the blade's back edge to resist rotation of the blade under load.*

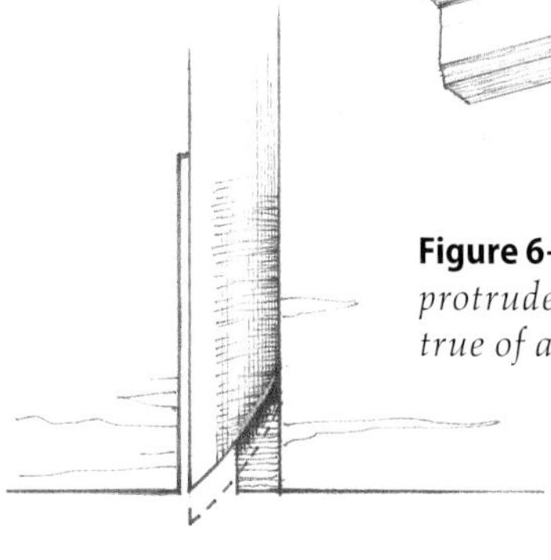

Figure 6-43. *The tip of the blade should not protrude below the bottom of the plane (this is true of all side rabbet planes).*

this, however, precisely at the point it reaches its own position at the edge of the blade. But with the resiliency of the wood dai, the chipbreaker has perhaps 1/16" (2mm) or more of play before it loses its grip on the blade, allowing the chipbreaker to work in a number of positions for different types of work.

Prepare the blade and chipbreaker as before, but do not yet adjust for pressure and a "four point" fit of the chipbreaker to the blade. Make sure the mating surfaces of the back of the blade and the edge of the chipbreaker are straight and flat. Install them and check the fit. Remove, and mark them both with

Figure 6-44. *The double-bladed side rabbet plane.*

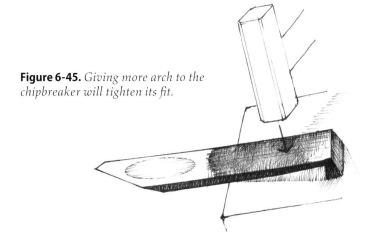

Figure 6-45. *Giving more arch to the chipbreaker will tighten its fit.*

graphite, ink, or Vaseline on the side that contacts the wood and insert. If they can be adjusted to working depth and have sufficient lateral adjustment, go ahead and true the sole and try a shaving. If not, remove them and see if there are marks on areas the full length of the bed, especially down near the blade. Pare the high spots away until you get bearing on all parts of the bed and they both can be adjusted to working position. If the fit is too loose, you can bend the chipbreaker a bit (above the hard blade steel!) by tapping it strongly with a small hammer on an anvil (Figure 6-45). You can also shim the blade or chipbreaker with paper glued to the bed or bearing surface of the chipbreaker. Once fitted proceed to truing the soles.

True the cutting face and bottom of the plane with a small plane. Once flat and straight, take a single shaving from behind the blade by placing the blade of the plane you're using just behind the mouth opening of the side rabbet plane and planing a stroke. Adjust the blade and take a trial shaving on a scrap of wood. Check the adjustability of both the blade and the chipbreaker. The blade should descend until its point is just flush with the arris of the cutting face and bottom of the plane, and the blade itself protruding from the cutting face a small amount and parallel with the cutting face of the plane. At the same time, the edge of the chipbreaker should be parallel with the blade edge and its point above or even with the point of the blade. If there is insufficient lateral adjustment, remove them both and pare the sides of the opening as required. If the pint of the chipbreaker is too long, you will have to grind its secondary bevel back (carefully), mimicking the angle it came with, until it is even with the blade point.

If chips jam the chipbreaker, you need to check the fit of the two: take them out and hold them up to the light as you would with a bench plane. Straighten them if they are curved where they come together. Check that the chipbreaker sits flat on the blade (Figure 6-46); if not file the high spot on the underside of the top of the chipbreaker until it sits flat. If the blade and chipbreaker are too loose after this, bend the chipbreaker a little to compensate.

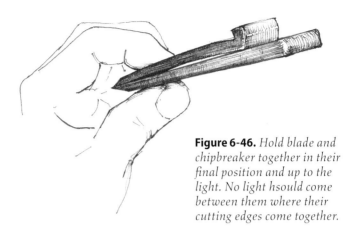

Figure 6-46. *Hold blade and chipbreaker together in their final position and up to the light. No light hsould come between them where their cutting edges come together.*

Setting Up Hollows and Rounds

The procedures for setting up hollows and rounds are followed in the same order as with the other planes, beginning with the inspection of the plane itself. Normally, the first step is to sharpen the blade. However, if you are altering the curve the plane cuts, or if you feel the current curvature of the blade is not correct, you should save this step until later, as noted below. However, since the blade must be fitted in its bed early on, flatten the back of the blade, just don't grind it to its final shape yet. Sharpen and fit the chipbreaker as described in the general procedures "Prepare the Chipbreaker" on page 70, and then prepare the blade seat as described in "Fit the Blade" on page 71. Prepare the sole as described below.

If you are setting up hollows and rounds, start with the hollowing plane first, as its convex sole can be shaped with a flat-soled bench plane or block plane. You can then use the hollowing plane to shape the concave sole of the rounding plane. Conversely, if you have a rounding plane of the same diameter or bigger already set up, you can use it to true the sole of a hollowing plane.

The procedure and theory for truing the sole of a rounding or hollowing plane is similar to that of a flat soled bench plane: two contact areas parallel to the curve of the blade contact the work in front of the blade (one immediately before the blade), and one (or more) parallel contact areas behind the blade in line with (or slightly relieved from) the contact areas in front of the blade.

Before starting, make an accurate template of the curve of the bottom. You can then use this to check your accuracy as you proceed. Use a straightedge held to the light to check

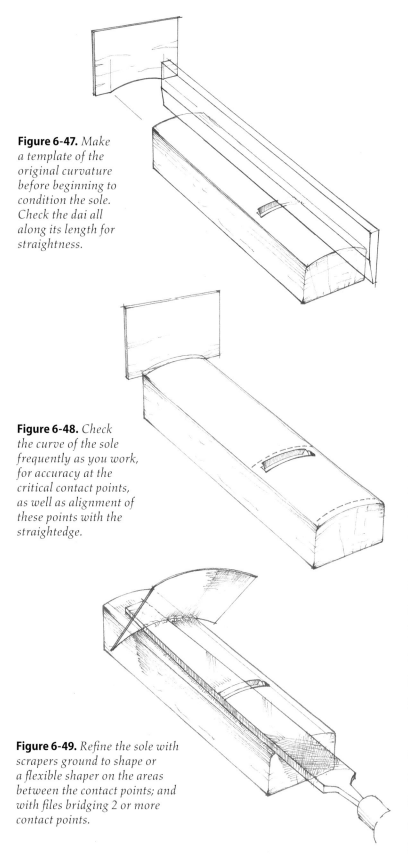

Figure 6-47. *Make a template of the original curvature before beginning to condition the sole. Check the dai all along its length for straightness.*

Figure 6-48. *Check the curve of the sole frequently as you work, for accuracy at the critical contact points, as well as alignment of these points with the straightedge.*

Figure 6-49. *Refine the sole with scrapers ground to shape or a flexible shaper on the areas between the contact points; and with files bridging 2 or more contact points.*

your contact points across the width of the plane (Figure 6-47); then using another plane with a very slight set on the blade so that it takes a very narrow shaving, plane the length of the hollowing plane, lowering the high spots until you have a straight sole and a consistent curve all across the width and the entire length (or use a coarse file). Use the template to check the profile all along, but especially at the front, back, and mouth (Figure 6-48). When the sole is straight and the profile is correct, you can fair and smooth the sole with a fine file. Use a light touch— you do not want to destroy the profile (Figure 6-49). Then you can come back and relieve the areas between the contact points with a curved or flexible scraper.

Check the blade and see if its profile matches the profile of the sole by inserting it in the plane and sighting down the sole. If it does not, you will have to grind the blade to match. Usually the blade is only slightly off, so trial and error in grinding, frequently checking your progress by putting the blade into the plane, is as efficient a method as any. If the discrepancy is significant, then marking the blade can be helpful. Though pencil is hard to read, it does not vaporize under the heat of the grinding the way a felt tip does.

After grinding, use your sharpening stones as you would for your other blades. Orient the blade to the stone in the usual manner, but use a rocking motion that rotates the edge through its entire length on each stroke. It is helpful to have a separate set of stones for this, as the convex blades will soon wear a hollow in the stone. I often take some of my old worn-out, or even broken stones, and dedicate them to curved plane blades and carving tools. Alternatively, you can use the edge of your sharpening stones, saving the face for your straight blades. Flatten the back as with other blades. You can use a hard buffing wheel to sharpen the edge, but use stones for the back. Do not be tempted to use the buffing wheel.

Shape the blade to a slightly different radius than the sole so that the blade tapers out to zero at the edges (Figure 6-50). This will keep the blade from leaving tracks or steps in the work.

For tuning up a rounding plane, with its concave blade and sole, after straightening the sole and sides, you can use a hollowing plane to reform the sole and round files to smooth it. You can use purpose ground scraper blades to finesse the relief areas and contact points. Grinding a concave plane blade takes a grinder that can access the curve. In a pinch, you can carefully use the corner of a grinding wheel, but it is hard to do good job. Ideally, you would use a narrow grinding wheel or one shaped with a diamond dresser to an appropriate curve. Alternatively, you can use a sanding drum on a drill press. Hone the blade; a diamond cone is ideal for the first stages of taking out the grinding marks because it will not wear and change shape as you work the edge. Then use slipstones to finish the edge. Scraps of broken Japanese waterstones or slipstones of the same material can be ground on a standard grinding wheel (the waterstones are quite soft) to shapes required.

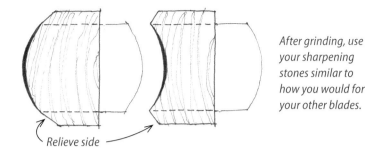

After grinding, use your sharpening stones similar to how you would for your other blades.

Figure 6-50. *The areas along the sole either side of the blade may have to be cut back at a greater angle in order to be able to fully access the hollow or round form you are shaping.*

On hollowing planes the sides of the sole must continue at least in the radius of the blade. Often they will have to be planed off at an even greater angle in order to access the cut on particular projects (Figure 6-50). On rounding planes, the sides of the sole may also have to be planed off at an acute angle to access work.

Troubleshooting

Using a handplane can be immensely rewarding, but it is not without its frustrations. Sometimes it seems you have done everything right but your results are still disappointing—or inconsistent. I cannot begin to answer all the questions you will ask yourself while you work, but a review of the information contained in this book should answer most of them. I will try to answer some basic questions here that I hope will tie information together and send you in the right direction when analyzing a problem.

Problem: The blade leaves a series of repeated parallel marks on the work, perpendicular to the stroke of the plane.

This is called blade chatter and happens

because the blade or blade edge is flexing under pressure of the cut. The edge digs deeper into the wood until the blade's resistance to bending exceeds the resistance of the wood, and the blade springs back up. At that the blade re-engages the wood, begins to flex, and the process happens all over again. Blade chatter happens primarily because the blade is not fully supported at the heel of the bevel, or because the bevel angle is too small (and thus the metal leading to the edge is too thin). There are a number of things to check, in the following order:

1. **Check that the blade is bedded properly.**

   Check the fit of the blade using the techniques you used to set up the plane. Check the bed, particularly at the sides of the blade under and near the area of the abutment. You should have a good fit here, as well as along the rest of the bed. The marking material should indicate that the blade is making substantial contact at all areas of the bed.

2. **The second most probable cause of blade chatter, and probably the primary suspect on a well set-up plane, is the bevel angle.**

   With a Japanese plane, I often check the bevel angle first, as I know how well the

EFFICIENT PLANING

If you use a too finely set plane to level the work, you must make many more cuts to bring the surface down to sufficient flatness. Each cut makes the blade a little duller. The use of intermediate planes reduces the number or strokes needed to level the work, thus reducing the amount of time, effort, and dulling cuts; and saves the edge on your finish plane for final smoothing.

blade is bedded, because I fit it in myself. The blades usually come with a 22° bevel, and this is often too small. If the bevel angle is too small, the bevel itself will flex and cause chatter. "Too small," however, is relative. The bevel angle must be appropriate for the depth of cut, the blade (cutting) angle, and the type of wood. For instance, a bevel angle may be just barely sufficient for a certain depth of cut, but may begin to chatter if set deeper, or if used to plane a harder wood. See the next section (#2, on bevel angle) for suggestions on how to address this problem.

3. **Another important factor related to the bevel angle is sharpness: When a blade dulls, it encounters greater resistance to the cut, causing the edge to flex down and begin to chatter.** You may notice this in the midst of working—the same plane that has been cutting well on the same piece of wood starts chattering and the only thing that has changed is the sharpness of your edge. This means your bevel angle on this blade is at the limit of its performance. You will have to keep this blade very sharp, or increase the bevel angle. If you suspect that the bevel angle is incorrect, or too small for the work you are doing, reconsider and adjust your bevel angles (see "Bevel Angle" on page 27 and "The Correct Bevel Angle" on page 26).

Problem: I cannot cut as fine a shaving as I want. The plane goes from a cut slightly too deep to no cut at all.

Either your plane or the work is not flat enough. Check the plane first—you probably have missed some area on the sole when you tuned the plane. This is easy to do. Go back and check it again.

The other factor is the work. If the work is not sufficiently well prepared, (not flat enough), you may have to set the blade deeper than you want to get the plane to cut even intermittent areas of the surface. If your plane does cut a fine shaving here and there, or maybe even at only one small place, then the problem probably is in the preparation of the work. You should go back and prepare it better.

Problem: I get tearout.

Using the information in this book, you should be able to see markedly improved results in the performance of your planes; with practice I hope you will find yourself planing woods and getting results you hadn't previously thought possible—and also knowing when to put down the plane and head for the scrapers and sandpaper.

The set-up of the plane is critical: a large portion of the skill required for effective planning resides here. Technique adds to this effectiveness, but does not compensate for it.

To reduce tearout, first, sharpen the blade. Match the blade steel to the work and make it—*sharp*. Use an appropriate blade pitch (if you can), adjust the chipbreaker and mouth opening to restrain the shaving, and use as light a cut as you can for the stage of the work.

If your plane and the surface of the work are well prepared, you can usually get

KEEP YOUR EYES ON THE PRIZE

The goal here is to get a beautiful surface suitable for the chosen finish and position of the piece in the work, in the most efficient manner possible. This is not an academic exercise. On the other hand, when you are learning about planes and trying to improve your skills, a little extra effort trying to figure out what is going on before turning to scrapers and sandpaper will be rewarded in the end. Ultimately, you have to decide when handplaning is no longer the most productive solution. Learning to make that decision is also part of the acquisition of skills.

A WELL-TUNED PLANE

I once watched a small 8-year-old girl take a full-width, full-length see-through-thin shaving off a cedar plank, 6" (152mm) wide by 6 feet (183cm) long, in one single continuous stroke—on her first attempt. The plane was a Japanese temple builder's 8" (203mm)-wide finishing plane that had been setup by a master carpenter. She walked backward pulling the plane with two hands while he walked along following her with a single finger kept lightly on top of the plane behind the blade to keep a consistent pressure on the work and to prevent her from flipping the plane off the plank. Probably the little person's skill was not yet highly tuned—but that plane certainly was.

good, reliable, tearout-free results on the final surfacing in most woods, though there will be those pieces that defy your best efforts. It is much easier to get tearout-free results when the plane is sharp, set for a fine cut (this has lately been proven by scientists researching the problem), but in order for this to work, the surface must be ready for a fine cut; that is, properly prepared.

Avoiding tear-out is a much bigger problem when preparing stock because preparing stock means removing a lot of wood, which necessitates a deeper cut, with the chipbreaker and mouth opening set back accordingly. The set up, of course, diminishes the effectiveness of these two major tactics in eliminating tearout. As preparation proceeds, you can gradually adjust the chipbreaker and mouth openings down to restrict the shaving, also taking a lighter cut. At each stage of the preparation you want to see tearout improve, aiming for its total elimination by the final smoothing.

Avoiding tearout also entails reading the wood and changing directions as you move across the surface accordingly. You learn the character of your wood as you plane, and you respond. Curly areas that change direction in the middle of the board may necessitate rotating the plane as you approach that area, to change the angle of attack, and then rotating it back again. Planing adjacent boards where the grain direction changes at the glue line often requires that you plane along the glue line in each direction without bridging the joint. Holding the plane at a bit of a diagonal localizes the cut a bit more and sometimes helps to be able to skirt along the joint.

KEEP THE SURFACE FLAT

Do not get distracted with localized problems. You must plane the entire surface the same amount—difficult areas as well as straightforward—in order to maintain flat. Otherwise, not only will the surface appear irregular but also the plane will begin to bridge the troubled areas by riding on the adjacent, less planed surfaces. These higher areas will then have to be planed down in line with the low areas before you can go any further.

Tearout hotspots notwithstanding, you should plane the entire surface in overlapping strokes across the width and length of the piece and back again. If you finish with scraping and sanding, do not be tempted to give trouble areas extra strokes, as this will distort the surface and be readily visible after the finish goes on.

A technique both Westerners and Japanese use is to dampen the surface of the wood with a wet rag to soften the wood fibers. This supposedly allows the fibers to be sheared cleanly. I have had mixed results trying this, and I suspect that it is not going to work in all woods, particularly those that prefer a higher cutting angle. I think it is worth further experimentation, however.

Problem: The mouth of the plane jams with chips.

First, take the blade out of the plane and check to see if the chips are jamming in the mouth itself, or at or under the chipbreaker. The chips may appear to be jamming at the mouth when in reality they are jamming at the chipbreaker and backing up to fill the mouth. This is the more likely occurrence.

If the chips are jamming between the chipbreaker and the blade, and not actually at the mouth, the chipbreaker's fit to the blade must be tuned so that it fits tight. The underside edge of the chipbreaker where it meets the blade must be straight, and slightly undercut (Figure 6-6).

If all of these are tuned up and chips still find their way in between the blade and chipbreaker, then possibly the edge of the blade is flexing under the pressure of the cut and opening up a gap between it and the chipbreaker. The bevel is flexing because it is too small (and thus the metal leading to the edge is too thin); or the blade is flexing because it is not properly supported. Sometimes the chipbreaker is rigid enough—and not tight enough—to allow a badly supported blade or too thin edge to flex independently of it. Check the bevel angle of the blade and consider regrinding it to a larger one if it appears questionable. As well, check the blade seat and make sure the blade is fully supported. Correct these and verify that the chipbreaker has enough pressure on the edge to maintain contact under working conditions.

Chips will also jam at the mouth of the plane itself because someplace there is insufficient clearance. Check that the blade is not set deeper than slightly less than the width of the mouth opening. Also, check the throat opening and the upper surface of the chipbreaker so there is sufficient clearance between it and all points of the chipbreaker. Sometimes if tolerances are very close, a blade will flex down into the wood in use and take a deeper chip than it was set for—than what the mouth or throat opening will accept. This is actually blade chatter, but since it happens only once and jams instead of leaving chatter marks, it is hard to diagnose this as the blade or blade edge flexing. If all the tolerances look sufficient, then check the bevel angle and blade support.

Problem: The plane leaves tracks or ridges in the work.

Rotate the work so the light source shines parallel to the work surface. Look closely and see if it is a ridge or a step. If it is a ridge, then you have a nick in the blade. You will have to go back and resharpen.

If the track is a step, then one or both corners of the blade are set too deep for the shape of the blade. You need to back the blade off or adjust the blade laterally until the blade no longer leaves steps. If it no longer cuts, then you need to either flatten the bottom of the plane some more or prepare the work better as described above. Check the different sections for the appropriate blade shape for the plane you are using.

Problem: The plane seems to leave shiny streaks on the work.

These are usually burnishing marks from some slightly higher spot on the sole of the plane. The most likely culprit is the area just to either side of the blade opening, since these are easy to neglect. This is why I relieve these areas on my planes; however, other missed spot on the sole can do this as well. Also, sometimes shavings can collect at the mouth (especially at the corners), pack tightly, and cause burnishing.

7

SHARPENING

Typical in the Japanese apprenticeship, the first

real woodworking task given to the apprentice

was sharpening his tools. Only when the

apprentice could demonstrate he could produce

an adequate edge did the master judge his skills

and his knowledge were sufficient to proceed. The

acquisition of skills begins with sharpening.

The ability to sharpen quickly and well is essential to the craft of woodworking.

Sharpening is fundamental to the craft of woodworking. Learning to sharpen fast and effectively lays the foundation for the acquisition of nearly all of the other skills to be required in the craft. It teaches body mechanics and the art of working efficiently. It teaches you how to focus both your attention and your efforts for maximum productivity. It teaches you to see, and what to look for. It teaches you to feel—to feel your own rhythms, the material, and the feedback from the tool—less smooth, smoother, smoothest, sharp, and sharper.

This is where woodworkers learn to make each motion pay off. You come to understand that the edge is not scrubbed back and forth across the stone but rather stroked with direct intention each time it is moved; that there is clear focus of effort, pressure, and attention at the cutting edge itself, not the bevel; and while the bevel does remain flat, not rocking on the stone, it is the edge of that bevel that's being sharpened and must be zeroed into with both the mind and the body.

Additionally, learning this and how to do it, and how to do it each time, makes it easier to understand other tasks; that each stroke of the plane is individual, dependent on the grain of the wood at that particular place, the angle of attack, your speed, your body position, the diminishing sharpness of the blade, and your increasing fatigue.

That sawing is not a tiring repetition of frantic arm motion but a series of individual strokes, each advancing the cut on the shoulder of the scribe line and to the maximum amount the wood and the cut of the saw will allow.

That clearing waste for a dovetail or mortise with a chisel is a series of distinct, clean, and precise cuts of exactly the same amount, to the line, so waste is cleanly excavated the first time to its final shape (though perhaps not its final size).

Understanding this—and eventually, with mindful practice, internalizing this—each stroke of the plane, the chisel, or the saw produces optimal results, and the work proceeds quickly.

Because of the importance of sharpening in teaching body mechanics and the art of working efficiently, I always strongly encourage woodworkers to sharpen without a jig. I also feel it is faster overall. Fortunately, the bevel on the thick Japanese plane blade is quite wide and it is relatively easy to feel this bevel when working and keep it flat on the stone. But this wide bevel will also teach you that pressure is not applied equally across the bevel. Because the edge steel is so much harder, if you apply equal pressure when honing, you will gradually wear away the softer backing steel quicker and the bevel will get thinner over time. It will also take you much longer to sharpen. You must apply greater pressure at the edge while keeping the bevel flat to the stone. But, you will find out, that this is true of all blades, especially if you want to shorten the time it takes to hone an edge.

Jig Drawbacks

Use a sharpening jig and your energy is dissipated, half of it going to the roller, half to the bevel, and very little going directly to the edge of the blade, which is where all of your energy should be going. The roller becomes a blindfold, obscuring your interaction with the edge you are sharpening. It keeps you from ever learning the feel of the bevel sitting flat on the stone as you stroke it; from learning to focus your attention at the edge, while keeping the bevel flat to the stone; from learning not to rock or lean yet, produce maximum results at that cutting edge where you want it.

Because the jig dissipates both your energy and your focus, effort is wasted and time is lost. It is slower, and it is disruptive. Add to that the problem of jigging the blade the exact position in the apparatus—because if it is not exact—not close but exact—you create a new bevel on the blade when you go to sharpen—and your time and tedium increase exponentially. Fortunately, a lot of jigs don't fit the short Japanese plane blade.

Learn to sharpen with the attention of the mind and body focused to your fingertips, because in the end, this will be how you will be doing woodworking. Yes, there is a learning curve, but really, woodworking is just one big learning curve. The challenges woodworking offers is one of its appeals. You can take a shortcut, but it will catch up to you later. Time invested here will serve you throughout your further woodworking endeavors.

Bevel Shape

The traditional Japanese blade with its hard, brittle edge steel must have a flat bevel—for several reasons. First, it gives maximum support to the edge while allowing the thinnest possible bevel. A hollow-ground blade undercuts the edge leaving little material to support it. It actually undercuts it more than you think because the actual angle is that of the tangent of the hollow just behind the edge. This is much smaller than the angle the blade was ground to (i.e. the angle of the tool rest at the grinder) and often results in a support angle behind the edge of much less than the 20° to 22° generally considered to be the absolute minimum practical bevel angle (see "Honing a Hollow Grind Bevel" on page 28). Telltale indications the bevel is not working are chattering (even though properly bedded, the undercut metal leading to the edge is flexing under load); clogging at the mouth or throat of a properly adjusted plane (the blade—not sufficiently supported by the bevel—is flexing down under load, enlarging the mouth, causing it to cut a shaving larger than the opening can accommodate); or clogging between the blade and the chipbreaker, even though is the chipbreaker is fitted properly (again, the blade's thin edge is flexing under load and opening a gap between it and the chipbreaker).

A flat bevel provides the thinnest possible edge with the greatest support behind that edge. If any of these problems show up with a flat bevel, it is because the bevel itself is ground at too small an angle, a geometry that is plain to see and easy to deal with. Additionally, because the hard, brittle steel is too vulnerable without the support of the bevel behind it, it can actually chip; that is, it will dull really quickly and quite a lot.

Besides its potential functional problems, I have always believed the hollow grind presents maintenance problems as well. A grinding wheel leaves deep scratches, many of which seem to remain even after establishing a brightly honed bevel. Most grinding wheels are 60 or 80 grit; under a microscope the grooves left by the abrasive look like the Grand Canyon next to the pattern left by a 1,200-grit sharpening stone. It is easy to hone what looks to the naked eye like a polished bevel and still have some of these deep grooves left. To ensure they no longer remain near the edge, I always give the bevel a few extra strokes on the first sharpening stone. However, waterstones cut so fast—much faster than the old oil or Arkansas stones— that this nearly eliminates the hollow. After two or three sharpenings, the hollow has been honed away. I could never understand the point of taking the time to regrind the hollow when the waterstones cut so fast. Now, let's get back to working wood.

There are some occasions, however, when I purposely establish a hollow grind, even if an edge does not have to be reshaped (because of a nick, for instance). The primarily reason is to take the hump out of a rounded bevel. Sometimes, after a number of honings, I just lose it. The bevel is simply too rounded to easily flatten. In such a case I put it on a grinding wheel and hollow-grind the area between the edge and the heel of the bevel. I do not take it all the

way out to the edge, both for expediency, and to avoid possibly overheating the edge. I grind away just enough that the blade sits flat on the sharpening stone and does not rock. I can then easily hone the blade to a flat, unrounded bevel. At the first honing, however, I do not necessarily take the time to fully remove the hollow left by the grinder. I just hone until the edge is sharpened. If a bit of the hollow remains, it is not enough to compromise the functioning of the blade, and it will be gone soon enough in the next honing or two, anyway.

A *rounded bevel*, usually a result of rocking the blade when sharpening, is also not desirable. It results in a much thicker bevel angle at the cutting edge, even though the average of the bevel overall may be the intended angle. A little bit of this (a very little) is acceptable and almost inevitable when sharpening by hand (I talk more about this a little further on). But too much results in the blade ceasing to cut at the least bit of dulling, as the bevel behind the edge begins to rub and suspend the edge from the work.

The *micro bevel* is, again, a maintenance issue with me. The micro bevel gives a good edge the first time. The next time you sharpen, you have two choices: sharpen only the micro bevel, or sharpen the whole bevel and the micro bevel. If you sharpen only the micro bevel, after two or three sharpenings, you will have a macro bevel. You will have lost all of the advantage of a micro bevel, and you have a main bevel that is rapidly developing a rounded profile. If you hone the main bevel to get the best edge, you must hone it all the way out to the edge, not just to the beginning of the micro bevel. Then, putting a micro bevel on the blade at this point is just redoing work

Anyway, if you hone without a guide (as I recommend), some slight variation in the bevel angle is unavoidable. In addition, with proper technique you can make this work for you. By rotating the blade orientation to perpendicular to the length of the sharpening stone on your final stone, rather than using the approximate 45° orientation that gives the most stability when sharpening, you assume a position of higher risk (Figure 7-1). The slight increase in inaccuracy will ensure the edge itself is polished and slightly bolstered.

I believe many of these elaborate systems—hollow-grinding, micro bevels, jigs—do not address one of the main issues of sharpening: its frequency. If you are using your planes to their maximum benefit, for periods, at least, you may have to resharpen several times a day—maybe every 15 or 20 minutes at some point in some projects. Fiddling with contraptions and a variety of angles each time consumes too much time and is distracting. Without all this stuff, but with a good set of stones and a properly established bevel angle, you can be back to woodworking after three or four minutes at the stones, which is sometimes less than the amount of time it would take to get a jig properly attached.

Figure 7-1. Position of Least Risk.

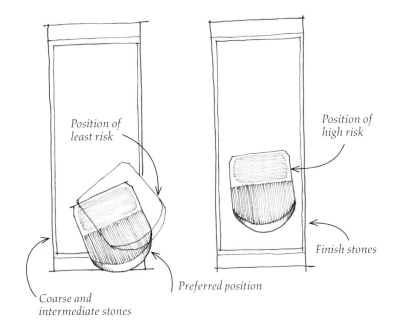

Position of least risk

Position of high risk

Finish stones

Preferred position

Coarse and intermediate stones

GRINDING OUT A NICK

Do not remove a nick by grinding the bevel; grind perpendicular to the edge. After removing the nick, grind the bevel until it just reaches the edge. If you grind out the nick by grinding the bevel, you are always working at the thin edge. This thin edge has no mass to help dissipate the heat, and is therefore at greater risk for overheating.

Grinding

I was once told never to grind a Japanese blade. Boy, getting a nick out of a blade without a grinder can be very Zen. I became enlightened, however, when a Japanese chisel maker told me that, yes, you can grind a Japanese blade on a grinding wheel—with the proper technique. The technique is simply to keep a finger directly behind the bevel, as close to the grinding wheel as possible. When the blade becomes too hot for your finger, it

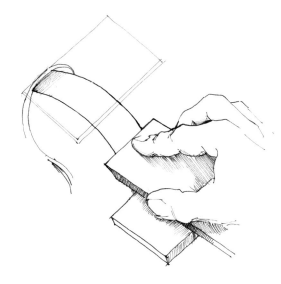

Figure 7-2. *Keeping a finger at the edge directly behind the bevel will tell you when the blade is becoming too hot. If the blade is too hot for your finger, it is too hot for the edge.*

is too hot for the blade, and grinding pauses (Figure 7-2).

While a grinding wheel can easily draw the temper of an edge, especially if the wheel is glazed, stopping short of changing the color of the edge, is still too hot. Aggressively grinding, stopping just short of color change, quenching, and then regrinding, causes noticeable structural change in the edge. Especially when combined with quenching, which itself can cause microscopic cracking. All of this degrades the edge, reducing the cutting ability and life of the edge. Both for the time it takes and for the risk involved, it is a good idea to grind as little as possible.

GRINDING ON A SANDING BELT

The natural tendency of a sanding belt is to round the pieces being sanded at both the approach to and exit from the piece. Reshaping the platen to give it a slight convexity compensates somewhat, reducing rounding at the approach and exit. Any remaining deviation from flat is little enough to easily remove when honing. Alternatively, a partial hollow can be established within a few seconds by putting the blade on the end wheel (in which case you will need a tool rest there as well), just enough to establish good registration on the stones and speed honing to the edge.

At some point, you will have to reshape a blade edge. For this reason, some sort of grinding device is indispensable. The power-grinding wheel is the most common, and probably, all things considered, the most practical. Get the slow-speed version (1,750rpm or so) and 8" (203mm) wheels for less undercutting of the edge. Keep the wheels trued and clean. Keep your finger behind the bevel, and work patiently.

ALTERNATIVES

An alternative to the grinding wheel is the standing stationary belt sander, about 2" (51mm) wide. Knife makers and many metal workers prefer them. They cut aggressively but have less tendency to overheat because the sanding belt carries away much of the heat. (You still can be too aggressive and overheat the blade, but it is much harder to do than with a grinding wheel.) This machine allows you several options for shaping the bevel. Besides the flat platen that produces a (nearly) flat bevel, usually you can work at one of the end wheels of the belt and achieve a hollow grind. The machine I have has an 8" (203mm) wheel that is usable. In addition, most machines have an arbor at the other side of the motor, which can be fitted with a grinding or buffing wheel.

Water grinding stones guarantee no heating of the edge. They tend to be slower (though not much) than power grinding or sanding, but they leave a great edge with little risk to the blade. They are, in some respects less versatile. You cannot do general reshaping tasks, such as grinding a new blade profile (as for a molding plane). On the other hand, the horizontal water grinder can sharpen power jointer and plane blades, something other grinders cannot easily do. Also, the horizontal wheel leaves a dead flat bevel, which no other grinding wheel does. It does need more maintenance than the others, though. The stones quickly wear and require frequent truing.

Vertical water grinding wheels have the same advantage as the horizontal water wheels. There is no risk of heat damage to the tool, but they leave a hollow grind. It is a matter of preference as to what shape you want behind your edge. Most of the wheels are much larger than most dry grinding wheels, so edges are undercut less. In addition, some of the systems seem quite elaborate—and expensive—and, considering you will probably have to get another system for the shop's other grinding/shaping tasks, the cost seems downright luxurious.

Sharpening Stones

It was not that long ago that Western woodworkers did not have many options for honing the edges on blades. Man-made oilstones or Arkansas stones were pretty much it. Oilstones were messy. They still clogged with debris, decreasing their effectiveness, despite all of the oil that was supposed to float away the debris. In addition, flattening them was impossible, and they did not cut very fast. Arkansas stones, a natural stone, were a step up, but the quality of the stones varied widely, and getting good quality

stones in recent years was increasing difficult as many of the best stone material has been mined out. And they shared many of the problems of the oilstones.

In the 1970s, manufactured Japanese waterstones became available, and they have revolutionized sharpening. Since then, major strides have been made in the quality and type of product available. American manufacturers now make waterstones, and by reports, their product is equal to, if not better than, some Japanese stones. I cannot keep track of all of the different stones. I have

Figure 7-3. *Besides using a straight edge to check the stones for flat (which I find difficult when the stones are wet), you can check by using your flattening stone, which in this case is a diamond stone. A few strokes with the flattening stone will reveal the hollow, stained with the iron removed in sharpening.*

Figure 7-4. *Here the stone is almost restored to flat.*

Figure 7-5. *Flat once again.*

settled on a number of stones that serve my needs, so I have not experimented widely with the different ones available. I suggest you consult the woodworking magazine reviews for comparisons of products and systems.

Nevertheless, you have to take some of the tests they do with a grain of salt. It is not simply a matter of which is the best sharpening stone, or the best sharpening system, but the best match, blade to stone. Though I have no verification for this, I suspect the technique used also is a factor in the effectiveness of different sharpening stones. I would not lose sleep at night over matching stone to blade, but some broad categories can be delineated. The clearest distinction can be made between the alloy steels and the carbon steels. Waterstones are much less effective on many of the alloy steels. On some alloys, waterstones do not really cut at all. If your waterstones seem ineffective on your alloy blades, you will have to use diamond stones and/or paste.

After that, determinations become much more subtle. The Japanese craftsman, intimately familiar with the character of his tools, will prefer different stones for different tools, because he knows that certain matches yield better results. For the rest of us, at least to start out, I would suggest a 1,200-grit stone to start followed by a 3,000- or 4,000-grit intermediate stone, finishing up with a 6,000- to 8,000-grit stone, or finer. If you have a very fine, special Japanese blade you may eventually want to consider getting a good-quality natural finish stone, as

USING AND MAINTAINING WATERSTONES

Before use, synthetic waterstones need to be soaked for at least 10 minutes, or until air bubbles stop coming out of the stone. If they do not have a wood base, you can store them indefinitely in water. A large lidded plastic tub is good for this. If they have a wooden base, you can still store them in water, but eventually the base may fall off. Synthetic finish stones (#3000 and above) generally do not need to be soaked, but check with the manufacture and/or dealer.

Natural waterstones are never stored in water because doing so causes them to disintegrate. Coarser stones are soaked for five or 10 minutes before using and removed after sharpening. The natural finish stones generally do not need to be soaked, but again check with the seller. Natural stones will often crack, by the way, if they are allowed to freeze, whether dry or in water.

The stones will have to be trued before they are used the first time and frequently as they are used. There are a number of ways to do this. My favored approach now is to use a diamond stone rubbed against the waterstone. I have been using the same diamond stone now for more than ten years and it has not worn out yet, so it is cost effective. Alternatively, you can use sandpaper—220-grit wet/dry on a piece of ¼" (6mm) plate glass laid on a flat surface.

However, you will get only about two flattenings before the sandpaper wears out, so costs can add up. In addition, sandpaper tends to glaze some stones (such as the Bester), so it is not always an option. I have also flattened stones on a concrete block, which works fine until the concrete becomes polished and the block wears out of flat. Also, a special stone is sold just for flattening sharpening stones, which works fine, but eventually it too gets glazed and out of flat.

Some stones are harder than others, so the frequency of flattening will vary. Frequency also varies according to the task. A good procedure is to sharpen your finest smoothing plane blade first, right after flattening the stones. Then follow in order with blades of increasing edge curvature, right down to the jack. That way you can actually use the wear of the stones to help shape the blade edges. You can even set aside old badly worn stones to hone blades of significant curvature (like a scrub-plane blade).

In use, coarser stones are periodically washed clean and kept wet by adding a bit of water from the soaking container. The blade is abraded directly against the stone. The finish stones are kept barely wet, but not allowed to dry out; the slurry is allowed to build up, as this is what actually does the polishing, not direct contact with the stone. Using a *nagura* stone (a chalk stone available where waterstones are sold) raises the slurry more quickly.

recommended by a good dealer and as your pocket will allow.

A few other sharpening materials can be useful. I have mentioned diamond stones. These are particularly useful for flattening the back of blades, as you can hone on them almost indefinitely without wearing them out of flat. With a waterstone, if your blade back needs a lot of flattening, the waterstone soon wears out of flat and will have to be flattened again. If you wait too long to do it, the curve of the stone will be honed into the back of the blade, so using a non-wearing "stone" is helpful here (Figures 7-3, 7-4, 7-5).

If your plane blade back is badly out of flat, it may be faster to use carborundum on an iron plate (*kanaban*) to flatten it. The iron grabs the carborundum and keeps it from grinding the plate (though it will wear out eventually and have to be replaced). (See "Flattening the Back of a Plane Blade" on page 65.)

SHARPENING

Years ago, a young man apprenticed to a furniture maker in Japan showed me this sharpening technique. It has served me well. I suspect it will do likewise for you.

Before beginning to sharpen, first find the bevel. You do this by putting one or two fingers down on top of the blade directly opposite the bevel, while simultaneously tilting the blade up with a single finger of the other hand underneath. Tilt the blade up and down with this finger while keeping pressure down on the bevel with the other hand until you can feel the blade rest securely on the flat of the bevel **(Figure 1)**. Do this exercise every time before you start sharpening, and several times during.

Similar to the exercise, when sharpening, the first one or two fingers of the off hand—the left if you're right handed—finds and maintains a steady pressure down on the bevel. At the same time, the right hand lightly grips the blade with the thumb and second finger, maintaining the angle, with the first finger applying downward pressure on the bevel (along with those of the left hand). The third and fourth fingers are lightly wrapped underneath. The number of fingers in each position may vary as sharpening proceeds, but the basic positions of the first fingers of each hand putting pressure on the bevel with the rest of the fingers of the right hand maintaining angle of the blade remain the same **(Figure 2)**.

An alternative grip is to put the right thumb under the top of the blade, supported by the left thumb **(Figure 3)**, and the rest of the fingers in about the same location as described before. While the broad bevel of the thick blade does make it a little easier to keep it flat on the stones, this is a position of higher risk and I usually use it only on the finish stone.

When moving the blade back and forth over the stone, the finger(s) of the left hand maintain a constant pressure down on the bevel to make sure it stays in constant contact with the stone. The right hand generally does the moving, assisted by the left hand though neither hand does only one task: they each assist the other.

Listen to and feel the bevel: when you sense you are no longer holding the bevel in constant contact with the stone—stop, relax your hands, do the exercise of finding the bevel, and start again.

Figure 1. *Before beginning to sharpen, first find the bevel. You do this by putting one or two fingers down on top of the blade directly opposite the bevel, while simultaneously tilting the blade up with a single finger of the other hand underneath. Tilt the blade up and down with this finger while keeping pressure down on the bevel with the other hand until you can feel the blade rest securely on the flat of the bevel. Do this exercise every time before you start sharpening, and several times during.*

Special Note: *Do not* attempt to steady the blade by putting fingers on the stone and dragging them along as you sharpen. This will soon cut through your fingertips, though you will not feel it until after it has happened, resulting in a painful, slow-to-heal wound.

Once you have had some practice sharpening and have gotten a better feel for keeping the bevel, you can begin working on an advanced technique. This is to actually put the focus of the sharpening effort right at the edge while still keeping the bevel flat on the stone when sharpening. It took me a while to discover this: after I got proficient at

Figure 2. *Similar to the exercise, when sharpening, the first one or two fingers of the off hand—the left if you're right-handed—finds and maintains a steady pressure down on the bevel. At the same time, the right hand lightly grips the blade with the thumb and second finger, maintaining the angle, with the first finger applying downward pressure on the bevel (along with those of the left hand). The third and fourth fingers are lightly wrapped underneath. The number of fingers in each position may vary as sharpening proceeds, but the basic positions of the first fingers of each hand putting pressure on the bevel with the rest of the fingers of the right hand maintaining angle of the blade remain the same. With the longer Western blade, the hand must wrap over the top of the blade. This makes the correct height of the sharpening stones especially important, as a too-high position will result in an awkward turning of the wrist when sharpening. These blades are also trickier as they are thinner and the bevel gives less of a support base, and the long blade makes it easy to lever it out of the correct angle.*

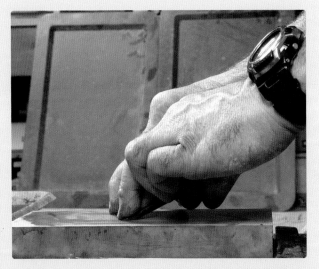

Figure 3. *An alternative grip is to put the right thumb under the top of the blade, supported by the left thumb (Figure 3), and the rest of the fingers in about the same location as described before. While the broad bevel of the thick blade does make it a little easier to keep it flat on the stones, this is a position of higher risk and I usually use it only on the finish stone.*

keeping the bevel flat, I noticed that over time the bevel angle on my laminated blades was getting smaller. I finally figured out that because the edge steel is harder than the backing steel, equal pressure across the bevel will wear away the softer steel quicker eventually making the bevel angle smaller.

To compensate, I concentrated my pressure when sharpening on the edge itself, while still keeping the bevel flat to the stones. Blades suddenly became sharper a lot faster. To do this, the right hand that supports the blade gives a little bit of pressure—focus—on the cutting edge itself by increasing the support it gives underneath the end of the blade while simultaneously concentrating the front fingers on the edge. I could say something like "the right hand lifts the end of the blade imperceptibly" instead to describe this, but this would give the wrong impression: it is an upward pressure there coupled with focused pressure at the blade's edge (rather than just the bevel). The blade is never actually lifted because this would round the bevel.

The required bit of curvature across the blade can be put on a smoothing plane blade by alternately putting pressure on each corner of the blade with the fingers that reside

SHARPENING *(continued)*

above the bevel. This is done three or four strokes at a time, on each stone. Similarly, pay attention to the distribution of pressure with the fingers. Unequal pressure may result in an unexpected and unwanted blade shape.

A dull blade has a blunt edge that is actually visible. To see it, you have to hold the bevel up to the light so that it catches the light. Then rotate the blade edge toward you until the reflection disappears. If you look closely, in this approximate range of rotation, the edge itself will light up. This may be very subtle, especially if the blade is not that dull, and you may have to rotate the blade back and forth gently to catch the light, but on a dull blade it is there. It's actually light reflecting off the plane of a dull edge: if a bevel comes together perfectly sharp, there is no place for the light to reflect off of. This reflection is called the "line of light." The work of the first stone is to eliminate the "line of light." Wash and dry the blade and look for it after you feel you've worked enough on the first stone. If it is still there, go back and work some more until it disappears.

The job of the subsequent stones is to polish out the edge that is established with your first stone. I was once told that time spent on each succeeding stone should be double that spent on the previous stone. Good advice—which I don't always follow in my haste to get back to work. Sometimes, if I spent much more time than I usually do on the first stone—because I let my blade get too dull!—I feel that doubling that extra time on the next stone will not be necessary because I have gotten good results in less time than that before. However, I have found that extended time on the finish stones usually results in a better edge than just "sharp" and is usually rewarded, on my best blades at least, with

Figure 4. *The back of the blade is lapped with a similar grip and pressure distribution as when doing the bevel: the right hands grips the blade with the thumb and second finger, with the first finger putting pressure on the very edge of the blade. The fingers of the left hand also put pressure just at the blade's edge. While the blade is never, ever lifted, the right hand does contribute an upward pressure at the off end of the blade while simultaneously focusing pressure down at the edge (Figure 4). The blade, of course, stays in solid contact with the stone the whole time.*

a noticeably sharper, better-performing edge.

The back of the blade is lapped with a similar grip and pressure distribution as when doing the bevel: the right hands grips the blade with the thumb and second finger, with the first finger putting pressure on the very edge of the blade. The fingers of the left hand also put pressure just at the blade's edge. While the blade is never, ever lifted, the right hand does contribute an upward pressure at the off end of the blade while simultaneously focusing pressure down at the edge **(Figure 4)**. The blade, of course, stays in solid contact with the stone the whole time.

Technique

I learned to sharpen on the floor. It has a number of advantages. You do not need to build a special table and have it take up space in you shop, and sitting, kneeling, or squatting can actually be restful to legs that have been standing all day. However, I do not seriously believe I can convince many people reading this to even try it, though I do highly recommend it.

What I learned from using this position is it is of little importance whether you are on the floor, sitting, or standing. What is important is the height of the stone relative to the body, and a solid, centered position that allows both movement and stability. The stone should be about 4" or 5" (102mm or 127mm) below the belly button. Lower than this and your will overextend your arms at the end of the stroke. Any higher and your elbows will be too bent and flailing about. Both positions will cause you to rock the blade on its bevel, rounding it over. Even if you use a jig, this is a good position, because it maximizes the energy of your movement.

Position yourself to maintain good solid balance even at the extremes of each stroke. If standing, have your feet apart, one slightly in front of the other. Feel the bevel lying flat on the stone and learn to recognize the feel and sound when the bevel loses full contact with the stone and rocks. Stop and feel the bevel's position again. Train your body to follow the bevel, to internalize the movement required to keep that bevel flat to the stone, and to maximize the expenditure of energy directly to the cutting edge itself. Have your mind focused on this cutting edge and this bevel in solid contact with the stone, with the body following in total attention and coordination. This is the beginning of skill.

8

HOLDING THE WORK

Certainly you can use a European style bench to hold the work when planing with Japanese planes. Over many generations, European cabinetmakers developed a very sophisticated bench for holding work that was to be planed and joined; when used along with its various accessories, it will hold pieces of almost any shape in virtually any of the positions that might be required to effectively work them.

A simple piece of plywood held in a vise can be used as a stop for the plane to work against.

The drawback I find to the classic European bench is it can be a bit cumbersome or slow when you have to plane regularly shaped pieces, especially when you have many of them to do. On medium-to-small size pieces, the time it takes to dog and undog a workpiece is roughly equal to the time it takes to plane a side. Thus, using the bench can double your work time.

Our predecessors noticed the problem. Specialty trades, for instance, often used much simpler benches and holding devises where work could be rapidly repositioned, with fresh pieces quickly replacing the finished ones. Craftsmen often worked by the piece, so speed was of the essence. If you did not have to take the time to turn a crank or vise handle to hold a piece and then turn it again to release it, you were saving time and energy, and making more money. Many of the trades were compensated barely above subsistence as it was.

Simple Stop

The vast majority of pieces the woodworker will want to smooth with his plane can be worked against a simple stop fixed to the bench. Although bench dogs and vises of the European bench are useful for holding workpieces while chiseling or shaping as well as planing, it is often not necessary to clamp regular-shaped pieces down to the bench with dogs or other clamping devices just to plane them. A workpiece can have its first side smoothed (if it is small, a side can be smoothed in a pass or two), flipped end for end (to maintain the best grain orientation), planed, then turned onto its side and planed, and then

flipped again end for end—all without having to reach for a vise handle. You can smooth a stack of parts quickly this way.

For planing, and even for much basic woodwork, you really do not need an elaborate bench. A stout plank with a stop fixed to it often will be the fastest and most effective way to hold the work. If the bench is only used for planing, this stop should be as wide as possible, not a single iron or wood peg, in order to handle boards of various widths without the pull of the plane causing the board to pivot away from you. The stop should preferably be a strip of wood fitted near the end of the planing board in a tapered dado or sliding dovetail so it can be removed or replaced.

The Japanese generally use a fairly simple bench. The building trades tend to use one or two heavy planks on trestles or saw horses for standing when working; these may be level, or if used especially for planing, sloped for more ergonomic efficiency. Furniture, and trades making smaller items, will have a plank set on the floor so they can work sitting down, and if used for planing, it is invariably sloped toward the user. These planks and their accessories are specialized according to the trade.

For planing, a simple peg, often fit tightly so that it can be tapped up or down, or a batten fixed across the plank is used as a stop. In the carpentry trades, in a pinch a nail or screw is used as a stop. In the furniture trades, often a couple of large pegs (2" to 3", or 50mm to 75mm, wide by ⅜" to ½", or 9mm to 12mm, thick) will be friction-fit near the end and somewhat toward either side of the bench. This allows room for other actions to happen on the bench. To shoot edges, a ledge may be installed along one edge to rest the plane on, essentially making the bench a large shooting board.

Work to be planed is not clamped, but is solely restrained by the stop. Vises are not often used in the trades, at least not traditionally, but I have seen the use of a vise for holding small parts used by one of the furniture trades. This looks and functions similarly to a hand screw or a European leg vise. One leg is mortised or bolted into the bench top with a stout tenon (so it can be removed) or a bolt. The other leg of the vise is free to move, but has a rod through it near its bottom that jams the active leg in position when pressure is put on the vise, and an acme screw and cross wheel at the top for quick clamping and release.

For a lot of woodworkers, especially those with restricted space, or a specific range of projects, a simple planning board as described above, used with a holdfast and a few vise-type accessories will be quite serviceable, and portable, and will probably serve the woodworker's planing and hand tool work quite well. The planing board can be as little as 3' or 4' long, depending on the nature of the work, and as little as only 9" (229mm) wide.

If you have a European-style bench, however, there are a number of things you can do to speed planing operations.

To avoid having to repeatedly dog and undog boards you want to surface-plane, or having to install a fixed stop to work against on your bench, you can simply clamp a short board in the tail vise so it projects above the bench top and plane against it (Figure 8-1). Or you can make up a stop of three pieces of wood or plywood to

Figure 8-1. *A board or piece of plywood put into the tail vise can be used as a planing stop for small and medium size pieces.*

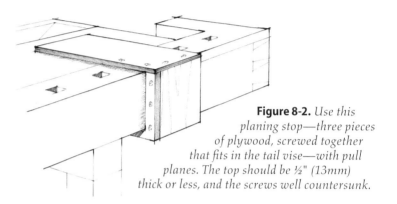

Figure 8-2. *Use this planing stop—three pieces of plywood, screwed together that fits in the tail vise—with pull planes. The top should be ½" (13mm) thick or less, and the screws well countersunk.*

clamp in the tail vise that will also handle wide boards (Figure 8-2).

For planing the edges of long, narrow pieces that will flex if not fully supported, I put a 4" (102mm) hand screw clamp in the tail vise (Figure 8-3). On the side of one of the jaws of the clamp, I have glued a strip of veneer (Figure 8-4). The veneer allows the other jaw to be adjusted freely when the clamp is held in the vise. When using the clamp, I first adjust it so the jaw opening matches the work it is holding. I position the clamp in the vise at a height that works with the piece I am planing (so it extends above the bench surface less than the thickness of the board being planed), tighten the tail vise to hold the clamp, and then the clamp to hold the piece.

For planing the edges of long, wide pieces, you can use the front vise to hold pieces up to around

Figure 8-3. *A handscrew clamp in the tail vise is a versatile clamp for holding work to be planed.*

Figure 8-4. *Glue a piece of veneer to the side of one jaw to provide clearance that enables the other jaw to be moved while the clamp is in the vise.*

Figure 8-5. *This European-style bench has peg holes in the legs and a traveling helper that rides on the top and bottom stretchers to help support long and wide pieces when edge-planing.*

5' (1.52m) long if they are not so narrow to flex when planed. Longer pieces will have to be supported. There arc a number of ways to do this. The first is to build a way into the bench. This assumes you are building your own bench or are willing to do some major modifications to an existing bench.

If making your own bench, build the legs flush to the front edge of the bench and drill a series of ¾" (19mm) holes in the front right leg to set a dowel or holdfast. The left end clamps into the front vise and the right end sets on the dowel or holdfast. You can drill holes in the left leg as well to aid in positioning large heavy work before fixing it in the vise, but it is not necessary. This works for pieces long enough to span from leg to leg. To accommodate shorter pieces, you can build two stretchers in the front, one low and one high, with runners on them to accommodate a traveling helper, similar to those found on Shaker benches. This is a board 6" to 8" (152mm to 203mm) wide with a series of staggered holes that slides back and forth on the stretchers (Figure 8-5). Some of the holes match the height of those you drilled into the legs.

If you do not have the option (or energy) to build or rebuild the legs on your bench, a portable helper can be made, several designs for which exist (Figure 8-6).

Probably the single most effective accessory for any bench, however, is the shooting board, or its cousin, the bench hook (Figure 8-7). I underestimated the usefulness of this tool for a long time but have gradually become more and more appreciative of its speed and versatility. The shooting board's first use is the trimming of ends of pieces, either square (probably most useful) or at a particular angle, such as 45°, done on a shooting board made just for this angle. Using a shooting board for trimming can greatly increase your accuracy. You can take off the thickness of a shaving, say a few thousandths of an inch with each stroke, giving you incredible accuracy, and because the stop supports the grain at the back of the strip, you do not have to worry about your piece chipping out at the exit side of the cut. (For more on making and using shooting boards, see my book *Getting Started with Handplanes*.)

We frequently associate these with push planes, but the stops can be reversed so that they can be used with pull planes, the rear underside stop hooked on the far side of the bench. The Japanese use a bench hook that's very similar, only the stop is more centrally located to accommodate the longer portion of the pull plane in front of the blade and a much taller vertical stop to provide a reference area for the plane. They may use a separate bench hook, longer, that they use for shooting. Also common are small bench hooks, U-shaped like a wooden miter box, that supports the plane front and back, and are used for trimming the ends of small pieces at a variety of angles (Figure 8-8). Generally the ends of pieces are worked with short, rather circular strokes, rather then the somewhat long straight strokes we might use in the West.

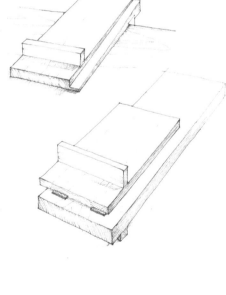

Figure 8-6. Bench Slave

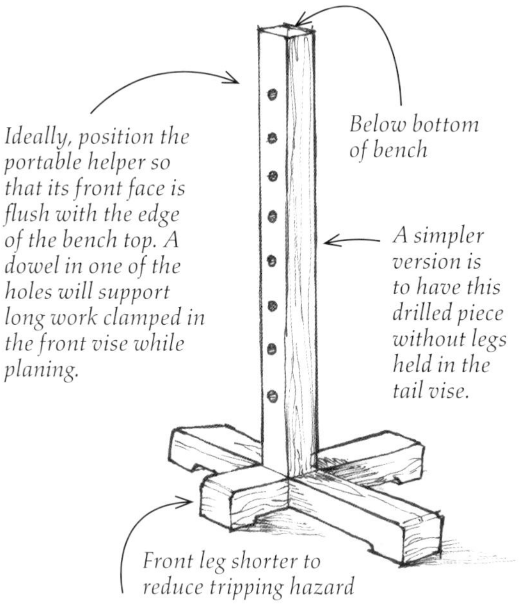

Ideally, position the portable helper so that its front face is flush with the edge of the bench top. A dowel in one of the holes will support long work clamped in the front vise while planing.

Below bottom of bench

A simpler version is to have this drilled piece without legs held in the tail vise.

Front leg shorter to reduce tripping hazard

Figure 8-7. Top *A Western-style bench hook with a sloped ramp, done to extend the wear area on the plane's blade. It is hooked over the back of the bench so it can be used with a pull plane. A bench hook without a ramp could be used with either pull or push planes simply by whether you hooked over the front or back of the bench.*

Bottom. *A Japanese-style bench hook on a planing bench. It is used against the bench's stops and can be used as a shooting board as shown, or slid over the edge of the bench to fully plane the ends of narrow pieces. Smaller pieces are planed in a gentle circular motion so that the blade edge is always coming at the work slightly diagonally shearing the wood grain.*

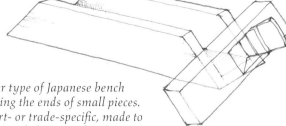

Figure 8-8. *Another type of Japanese bench hook used for planing the ends of small pieces. These are often part- or trade-specific, made to sizes and angles as needed. Again the plane is used in a kind of circular motion.*

A SIMPLE BENCH

Years ago, in the basement of a house I was renting, I came across a 4x10 (102mm x 254mm) beam in amongst some scrap lumber, abandoned by the previous tenant. It was 8' long, had a series of pairs of ⁵⁄₁₆" (8mm) holes drilled through the broad face down its length, and a ledger screwed along the whole length of one edge. Obviously, someone had intended this to be a workbench, perhaps in the Japanese style. However, as it was, it did not appear that useable to me. Nevertheless, the wood was a nice piece of fir, dry and straight. I used it for years as a portable bench on the worksite, supporting it on a pair of workhorses, and gradually became aware of its potential **(Figure 1)**.

I have since installed two removable stops of different heights at each end that slide in on tapered dovetails. They can be removed or moved to opposite ends as needed, with just a tap of the hammer. I need stops at either end because I use both push and pull planes **(Figure 2)**.

I installed a wooden hook near one end above the ledger similar to the hook on the Roubo bench in Scott Landis's *The Workbench Book* (Taunton Press, 1987). This allows me to set a board on edge on the ledger and push the end of the board into the hook (again, without having to clamp or use a vise) to stabilize it while shooting the edge **(Figure 3)**. The ledger along one side can also be used for shooting edges by setting the plane on the ledger with the board flat on the surface of the bench and using the bench as one large shooting board.

Into the holes, I inserted ⁵⁄₁₆" (8mm) dowels about an inch longer than the thickness of the bench. As it turned out, most fit snuggly, allowing me to adjust their height by tapping them up or down with a hammer. I generally do not use these as stops because they are rather small, but more for positioning alongside work to keep it from shifting

Figure 1. *The planing bench in its simplest incarnation, sitting on a pair of workhorses (Japanese-style, in this case).*

Figure 2. *Full-width stops are fitted into dovetailed grooves near either end, so that they can be easily tapped out and removed or exchanged. Holes have been drilled for holdfasts.*

Figure 3. *A similar hook (this from Roubo) could easily be rigged at the end of the bench for pull planes. I have also seen a ledger used with a flat-head screw, driven into the edge of the bench, as a stop. The screw can be adjusted in or out, or screwed down entirely to be out of the way.*

Figure 4. *Clamp a handscrew to the bench for use as a versatile vise.*

Figure 5. *A chairmaker's vise can be clamped to the top.*

Figure 7. *I added a tool shelf behind the work surface and added a slotted stop against which I can work. In order to keep the horses from rocking from heavy planing, I pressure-fit a lower shelf on the stretchers of the horses to lock in their placement, pressure-fit the tool shelf, and added diagonal braces. Half-lapped and notched at either end to tightly fit to the top rail and stretchers of the horses, these help make the whole assembly rigid. Moreover, everything disassembles without tools.*

to the side, because of either an irregular end or diagonal planing. If I had to do it over again I probably would make the holes ¾" (19mm) in diameter so dowels in them would be stout enough to use as stops, and then the holdfast could be used as well in the holes.

When I use the bench in the field, if I need to hold a piece for shaping or cutting, I clamp a large hand-screw clamp to the top at the end. This works quite well and, unlike many vises, will hold tapered pieces **(Figure 4)**. If I really wanted a vise, I would probably fix it to the end rather than the face, so as to not interfere with the ledge on the front. In addition, for holding pieces to be shaped, a chairmaker's vise (sometimes called a carver's vise) could be clamped to the top through one of the holes drilled through it, allowing a variety of positions along the bench **(Figure 5)**.

For some complex pieces and operations I still have to resort to my European bench, but for most planing operations I find this simple bench very versatile and much faster.

Figure 6. *The bench has seen adjustments and additions as I worked with it over time. I placed a couple of stout dowels in the bottom of the bench to fit into holes drilled into the workhorses to keep the bench from scooting around under heavy planing.*

Figure 8. *The planing bench at its home in the shop. When not being used in the field, the bench rests here atop my tool chests.*

9

MAKING AND MODIFYING PLANES

For a woodworker today, making your own planes allows you to

customize your tools to specific criteria and not be limited by what is

available commercially. Your planes can be larger or smaller than what

available commercially, with blade angles, widths, and lengths more

appropriate to the work you are doing.

Making your own Japanese plane gives you additional control over the bed angle and throat.

Figure 9-1. Grain Orientation.

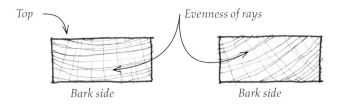

End View: Either orientation of the growth rings is acceptable.

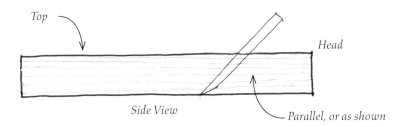

Figure 9-2. Blade Width.

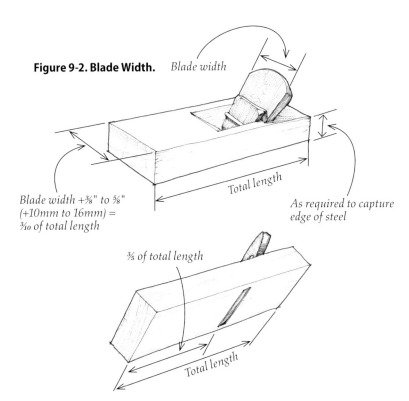

Making a Japanese-style Plane

Japanese-style planes, of all the styles of planes, can be the fastest to make, and, because there is no glue to dry, they can be used the same day. Moreover, the design is versatile and can be adapted to a variety of shaping and finishing requirements. Angles, widths, and lengths can be varied for finishing a variety of woods. Shapes can be varied for rough shaping or for finishing moldings or carvings. Anyone with good hand skills should have little problem constructing the basic plane.

First, obtain a blade of suitable width. If this is your first plane, start with a blade narrower than 55mm (2⅛"). Making planes for 60mm and 70mm (2⅜" and 2¾") blades is more difficult, increasingly so, the wider the plane. I find that 48mm (1⅞") is a versatile size and a good one to start with.

The block must be made of dense wood. If you have ever felt the difference between the white oak used for a dai and common Japanese white oak (similar to our red oak in density and texture), you will realize the density required: the oak used for the dai, both red and white, is considerably denser than the common stock. This is a result of trees carefully selected and cut just for the plane-making trades and involves a drying process often lasting two to three and sometimes 10 to 40 years. In addition to being dense and hard, the wood must also grip the blade well, which the wood of the Japanese dai does very well. For those reasons, I like to use the Japanese dai, which comes pre-cut to match your blade width. In a pinch, I have used cherry, beech, rosewood, canary wood, and angico. The last two were the most effective; I had trouble finding pieces of cherry and beech that were dense enough. A dense piece of indigenous white oak is also a good choice. Maple is not a good choice because, even though it is hard, it does not grip the blade well.

Orient the grain as shown in (Figure 9-1). Grain orientation is important if for no reason other than resistance to the wedging action of the blade. Select a dai that is ⅜" to ⅝" (10mm to 16mm) wider than your blade—a 48mm (1⅞") blade should have a dai that is 2¼" to 2½" (58mm to 64mm) wide. It should be thick enough to capture almost the entire hardened portion of the blade at the intended angle. Lengths are somewhat standardized on finish planes— the width being about three-tenths of the length—but this can be altered according to the intended use of the plane. Truing planes such as jointers are, of course, longer, but finish planes can be made much shorter to

facilitate the cutting action of a very finely set blade.

The edge of the blade is traditionally set at a point about three-fifths of the length of the plane back from what we would call the front of the plane (the Japanese call this the *back* of the plane, and the area behind the blade the *front* of the plane (Figure 9-2). This position is also not absolute, because on a shorter plane, you might not end up with enough wood behind the blade to support it, and so this area in front of the blade could be proportionally shorter.

Next, select the angle of your blade. Japanese plane blades are frequently set at an angle of 8 in 10 (Figure 9-3), or approximately 40°. I have made finish planes at 9 in 10 (43°), 10 in 10 (45°), 11 in 10 (47½°), 12 in 10 (50°), and 53° (13 in 10). You may want to reread Chapter 2, the section on blade angles, before deciding. I have found the 9 in 10 (43°) blade angle to be very versatile.

Before laying out and cutting the block, you must flatten and sharpen the blade, as well as the chipbreaker if you are using one. (See Chapter 6, Prepare the

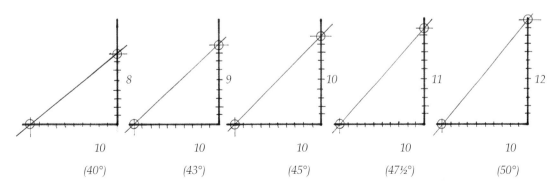

Figure 9-3. Traditional Japanese Method of Establishing Blade Angles and Their Degree Approximations.

LAYING OUT A BLOCK FOR A JAPANESE PLANE

1 Mark a line for the blade edge.

2 Use a bevel gauge to mark the angle of the blade, beginning at the blade-edge line. Transfer all lines around the block.

3 Mark the angle above the throat—the chipwell—at 45° to 50°, starting ¼" (6mm) above the bottom. Transfer the lines around the block.

4 Lay out the relief angle of the throat at 75° to 80° (more if the angle of your blade is high), and transfer the lines around the block if you wish.

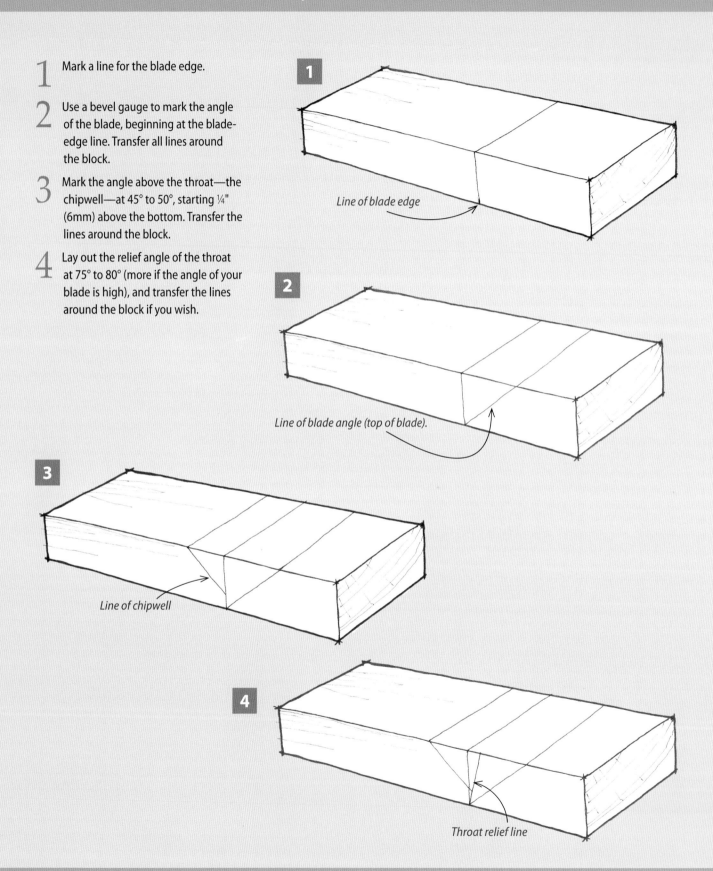

Line of blade edge

Line of blade angle (top of blade).

Line of chipwell

Throat relief line

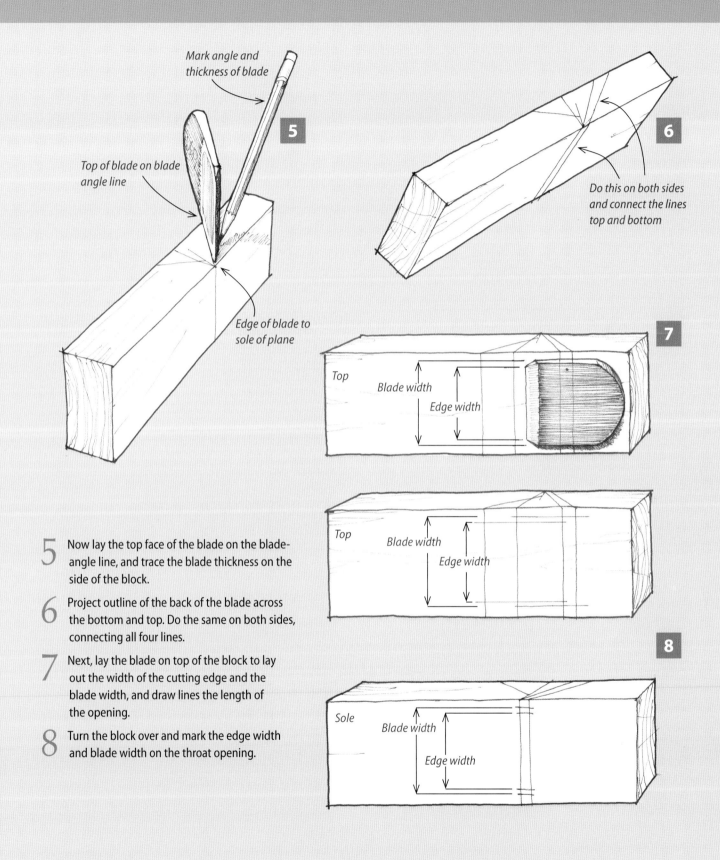

Mark angle and thickness of blade

5

Top of blade on blade angle line

Edge of blade to sole of plane

6

Do this on both sides and connect the lines top and bottom

7

Top

Blade width

Edge width

Top

Blade width

Edge width

8

Sole

Blade width

Edge width

5   Now lay the top face of the blade on the blade-angle line, and trace the blade thickness on the side of the block.

6   Project outline of the back of the blade across the bottom and top. Do the same on both sides, connecting all four lines.

7   Next, lay the blade on top of the block to lay out the width of the cutting edge and the blade width, and draw lines the length of the opening.

8   Turn the block over and mark the edge width and blade width on the throat opening.

Blade" and "Prepare the Chipbreaker" on pages 65 and 70, respectively.)

Now begin the layout of the block, making sure all edges are square. (See "Laying Out a Block for a Japanese Plane" on page 124.)

Begin making the plane by chiseling the top opening. Since I'm right-handed, I find it easiest to lay the block on my bench against a stop at the left end, chisel in the direction of the stop—sighting down the back of the chisel—and then rotate the block—rather than my body position—and chisel the other side of the opening. (See "Chiseling the Chipwell, Mouth & Blade Seat" on page 128.)

Once you have the blade seat prepared (see Step 7 on page 129) and the escapement cut that captures the blade (see Steps 8-11 on page 130), you can trial-fit the blade. Probably it will barely go in. (Verify also that you have extra room on either side for lateral adjustment.) Sight along the back of the blade to see where it is hitting. Hold the plane up to the light and sight between the blade and its seat; you should not see any light. Most likely, the blade seat will be too curved. If, when you begin fitting the blade, there is considerable light—a gross misfitting of the blade—you can pare down the obvious high areas before you begin the marking and paring process, thereby saving yourself some time and tedium. Flatten the bed along its length until the blade goes in about halfway, or until it begins to approximate the curve of the back of the blade. It is important to note that the underside, or bevel, side of the blade usually is forged to a concave shape

across its width. Coat the back of the blade with ink, pencil, or petroleum jelly, and slide it into place. When you remove it, the high places of the blade seat will be marked. Pare or scrape these down carefully and repeat the operation. It might be helpful to reread: Chapter 6, Step 4, "Fit the Blade" on page 71, which has a more thorough description of the process.

Continue removing material from the areas marked until you can push the blade in by hand up to a point about equal to half the width of the blade's bevel from its final position—or around ⅛" to ³⁄₁₆" (3mm to 5mm).

If, when you are doing the final fitting, you pare away too much, you can shim the blade using paper glued to the blade seat. Try a single layer of bond (printer) paper first— you will be surprised how much difference one piece of paper can make.

Turn the block over and finish paring the throat opening to the line. If this is to be a fine finishing plane with a chipbreaker, then this may be the entire opening you need because the pressure of the chipbreaker tends to open the throat slightly. If it is to be a coarser plane, or one without a chipbreaker, you may want to open the throat a little more. Tap the blade into its final position and look at the gap. Do this carefully—or you may drive the blade into the throat should there not be enough opening to begin with.

Fitting the pin for a chipbreaker is a little tricky. Put the blade and chipbreaker together, lay the blade top on your blade-angle layout line, and mark the line of the chipbreaker in the same way you marked the blade in the beginning (Figure 9-4). Alternately, you can use a bevel gauge set at the blade-angle, set the dai in a vise at the height of the bevel gauge so it rests securely, and then put the chipbreaker against it to mark. Mark a line about six-tenths of the way up from, and parallel to, the sole of the plane. The center of the pin lies on this line at a distance of one radius from the line marked for the top of the chipbreaker (Figure 9-5).

Bore in carefully from one side. Insert the blade and chipbreaker to their final position, and tap the pin in to check its fit. Hopefully, the fit will be close. If not, there are ways to correct it. Mark the line of the top face of the chipbreaker inside the plane as well as the line parallel to the bottom. Mark the center of the pin and bore the hole—inserting the bit through the first hole. It is not necessary to bore the hole all the way through. Insert the pin, blade, and chipbreaker, and check the fit. If the fit is too loose, bend the corners of the chipbreaker more. If the pin is too tight or not parallel, file it. If the pin is grossly off, the next larger diameter pin can be fit by using a rat-tail file to enlarge the pinhole in the direction needed.

Flatten and relieve the bottom with scrapers to the configuration appropriate to your plane. See Chapter 6, "Step 5: Configure the Sole" on page 74.

Finally, finish the rest of the plane. The leading edge of the plane and blade bed must be sharp and crisp in order to prevent loose

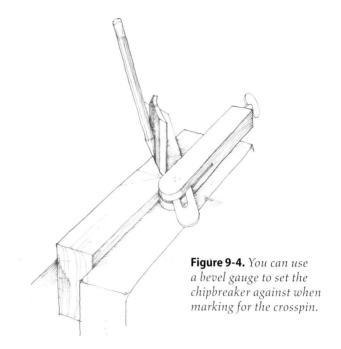

Figure 9-4. *You can use a bevel gauge to set the chipbreaker against when marking for the crosspin.*

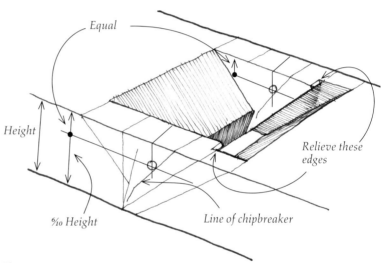

Figure 9-5.
- *Pin diameter ±³⁄₃₂" (2.5mm) for 40mm–45mm blade*
- *±¹⁄₈" (3mm) for 45mm–55mm blade*
- *±⁵⁄₃₂" (4mm) for 55–70 mm blade*

chips getting underneath the plane while working. I relieve the areas on either side of the blade (see Figure 6-17 on page 74) because these are hard to level in the course of maintaining the bottom and often become high spots that mark the work. I also chamfer both sides of the bottom to reduce some of the areas bearing on the work and thereby

CHISELING THE CHIPWELL, MOUTH & BLADE SEAT

1. Chisel to a clean V-shaped opening, keeping the cuts parallel to the blade-bed line and the chipwell line. You can chisel with the bevel down at first if you want, but as you progress, turn the bevel up and keep the back of the chisel at the same angle as the chipwell and blade-seat lines marked on the side of the block.

2. Do this by positioning yourself so you can sight down the back of the blade and along the lines marked on the side at the same time. It is important to maintain the proper angle of the cut, especially once you are within ⅛" (3mm) of the line. If you overcut the line at the blade seat, you will ruin the block.

3. Chisel the opening at the angles marked—approximately ⅛" (3mm) inside the front and back lines and 1/16" (2mm) inside the sidelines—until all lines meet.

4. Turn the block over and chisel the throat opening somewhat shy of the layout lines.

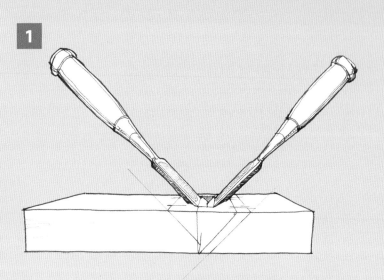

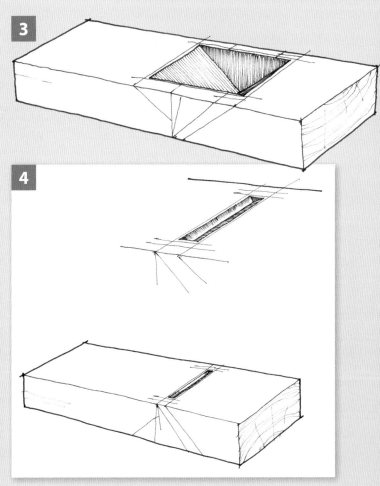

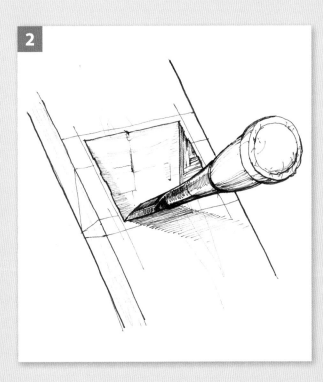

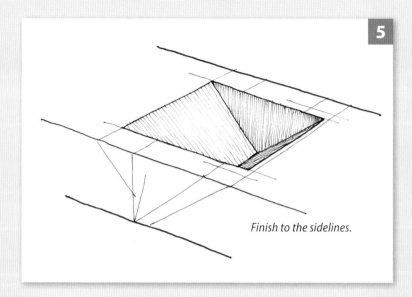

Finish to the sidelines.

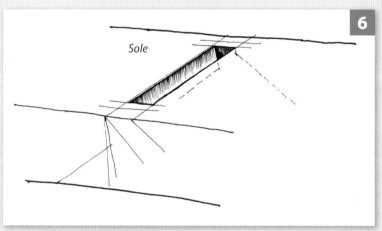

Sole

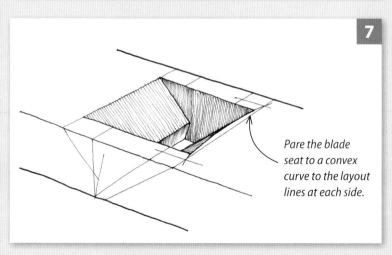

Pare the blade seat to a convex curve to the layout lines at each side.

5 Continue chiseling from the top, finishing to the line in front above the throat, but only to within +1/16" (2mm) of the back line (the blade seat), and at the proper angle.

6 Cut the throat open at its angle a little shy of the line—about 1/64" (0.4mm). Continue cutting until you break through. Clean up and finish from the top.

7 Pare the blade seat to a convex curve to the layout lines at either side.

CHISELING THE CHIPWELL, MOUTH & BLADE SEAT *(continued)*

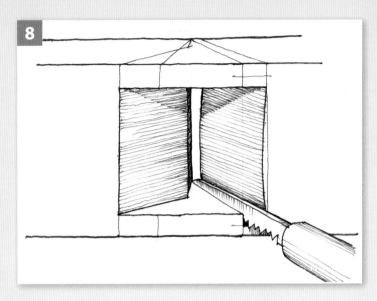

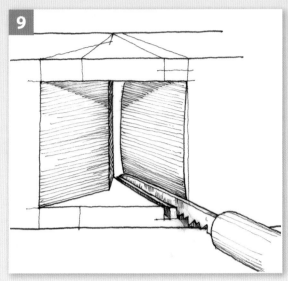

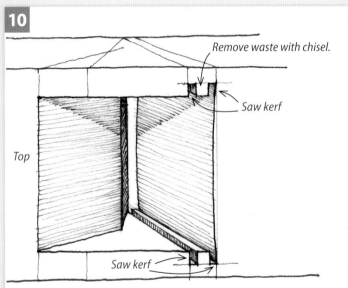

Remove waste with chisel.

Saw kerf

Top

Saw kerf

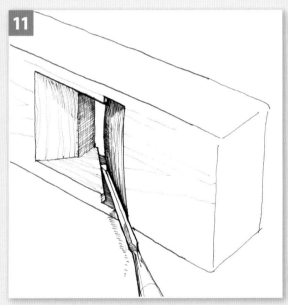

8 With a good quality keyhole saw, cut to the lines of the abutments that hold the blade. The blade-angle line (top of the blade) is critical—the cut must be straight and accurate. The cut is easier to start through the throat opening, starting the saw cut at the top of the block. Finish the cut from the top, making sure it is to its full depth.

9 Cut the blade seat line from the top by laying the saw on the blade seat.

10 After sawing, you will have a strip of waste between the kerfs on each side.

11 Clean out the cut to the lines with a small chisel.

lessen the friction. The top edges can be rounded all over, with the area behind the blade chamfered at an angle perpendicular to the blade and then rounded a little to reduce damage when the blade is being tapped out.

You can treat your block with oil if you like (Figure 9-6), using either camellia oil to reduce friction in use or tung oil for stability, but my personal preference is to skip this step. Rub the bottom with an oiler charged with camellia oil when the plane is completed, and frequently when working, making sure to lubricate the blade as well. This will not only reduce the friction of the sole, but also, the Japanese believe, extend the life of the blade's edge by reducing the heat caused by the friction of the cut.

Set the blade and try it, making sure you have clearance at the throat. You should get a shaving. If not, or if you cannot produce as fine a shaving as you want, and you can see the blade is protruding, then the bottom is not flat. Check again; assuming the blade is sharp, you missed something (Figure 9-7).

Making Chibi-Kanna

Making these small planes is the same as making the larger Japanese planes, but because the blades are small, the bedded side of the blade is flat and not concave, and because they are usually made without a chipbreaker, they can be made quickly. Refer to the other sections in this chapter for laying-out and making Japanese planes, and for laying-out planes with blades having a shaped edge.

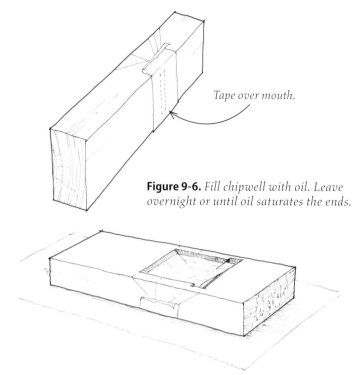

Tape over mouth.

Figure 9-6. *Fill chipwell with oil. Leave overnight or until oil saturates the ends.*

Figure 9-7. *The completed plane. Works pretty well.*

Traditionally, the blade stock for the *chibi kanna* (small plane) comes in about 4" (102mm)-wide sections (the blade length is about 2", or 51mm), and is available in different grades. It is a laminated piece of steel, like the material out of which the bigger blades are made, but having a gentle hollow grind from the edge to the upper portion of the blade where the lamination ends, and extending straight across the full width of the stock. This is done so that a blade of any width can be cut from the blank (Figure 9-8A) and still only the very edge has to be honed flat, rather than the entire back (Figure 9-8B). This long, gentle sweep of the hollow grind does not affect the fit of the blade in the dai; the blade is fitted in its tapered escapement, bevel down, much as other Japanese plane blades are.

To make a blade, you mark the required width, cut through the backing steel with a hacksaw, and snap the brittle edge steel free

Figure 9-8A. *Chibi-kanna with the blades removed. All of the blades in these chibi-kanna were cut from a larger blank, two of them from the blank in the foreground.*

Figure 9-8B.

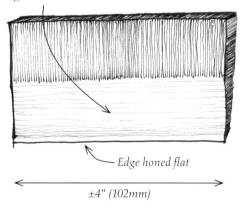

Inlaid edge steel; slight hollow ground across entire width

Edge honed flat

±4" (102mm)

of the larger blank (Figures 9-9 and 9-10). Grind the edges smooth and, if you wish, shape the top edge where you will be tapping it with a hammer for adjustment (I usually don't bother). Then hone the back of the blade. Because only about the last ¹⁄₁₆" (2mm) of the back, at the edge, is honed, it goes fast. Then, sharpen the bevel.

Alternatively, since this blade blank is hard to find, you can buy the small blades already cut and finished to width, and sometimes even with the edge shaped to one of various curves. These come in sizes from about ¼" to around ⅞" (6mm to 22mm) wide and about 2" to 2¾" (51mm to 70mm) long. These laminated high-quality blades hold a good edge.

Select the material for your dai. I often save the cutoffs from other planes I have made to use for these finger planes. The type of wood and grain orientation is the same as for the larger planes. The dai needs to be ¼" to about ⅜" (6mm to 10mm) wider than your blade. While you can, of course, make the planes any length, most of the time you want the plane proportionally short for the width of the blade, so it can get into restricted areas and easily shape or smooth what might initially be a less than perfectly level surface.

If this is the case, the finished length should be around 2" to 2½" (51mm to 64mm). Give yourself some extra length when first laying out your dai; you may need it after determining the position of the mouth. To determine the thickness of the dai, decide on your blade angle; the dai should be thick enough to capture the laminated portion of the blade. Check your blade, but this usually results in the dai being ¾" to about 1" (19mm to 25mm) thick.

The dai is laid out as with any Japanese-style plane, but because of its shortness, there are some layout parameters to remember. You need about ¼" (6mm) or more of dai behind the blade at the top to properly support the blade. Because of this, the layout of the dai begins at the back behind the blade to ensure you have enough wood there, rather than locating the mouth first at the usual three-fifths of the length of the dai. On a block longer than you think you'll need, begin your layout with a line, representing the top face of the blade, across the top back of the dai about ½" (13mm) in from the end. Then draw your blade-angle line from this to determine the location of the mouth. Depending on the final length of your dai, the mouth may end up being far forward of where you expected it. You do not want much less than half the length of the plane in front of the blade, or you will find it awkward starting a stroke. Cut the length of the dai after you have determined the position of the mouth (Figure 9-11).

Finish laying-out the dai. If you are making a plane with a curved blade, you may have to use the graphic projection method to cut the mouth opening. Most chisel blades are too thick to cut open the mouth at the angle of the blade as described in the direct cutting method. (See "Laying Out and Cutting the Mouth Opening for Hollowing and Rounding Planes" on page 141.)

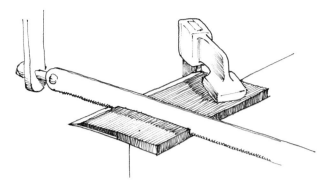

Figure 9-9. *Clamp the blank down and saw all the way through all the soft steel. You won't be able to cut the edge steel.*

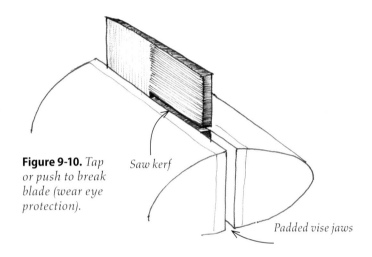

Figure 9-10. *Tap or push to break blade (wear eye protection).*

Saw kerf

Padded vise jaws

Figure 9-11. Laying Out Chibi-Kanna.

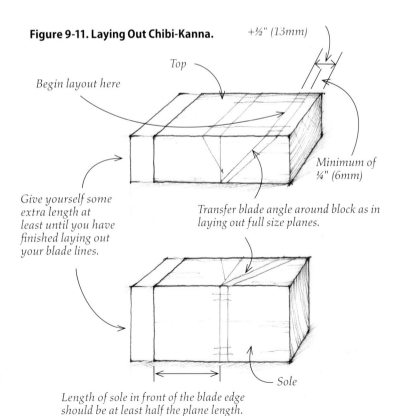

+½" (13mm)

Top

Begin layout here

Minimum of ¼" (6mm)

Give yourself some extra length at least until you have finished laying out your blade lines.

Transfer blade angle around block as in laying out full size planes.

Sole

Length of sole in front of the blade edge should be at least half the plane length.

To cut the dai, follow the same procedures as you would for a larger plane. If you are doing a plane with a shaped sole, first fit the blade most of the way to its final position before shaping the sole. When you are done with the sole, finish fitting the blade and adjust the mouth shape, if necessary.

Making a Compass Plane

If you are modifying a plane, make sure that the curve you are intending is not too severe; you do not want to remove too much wood (more than about a third of the original height of the plane body) and render the plane unworkable. This is especially true of a plane with a concave sole, as any more than a slight curve will open the mouth too much, encroaching on the throat area, and may reduce the bed of the blade too much, as well. If you want more than a slight curve on a concave-sole plane, you may have to make a new plane with dimensions to compensate for what will have to be cut away (Figure 9-12).

Make a template directly from the work or a full-scale drawing, or use a thin batten or a compass to make the curve. The curve must

be part of a circle (i.e., have a constant radius, not a varying radius, like a French curve). It is best to make a template of the curve of the work rather than the curve of the plane; that way you can use the template against the plane to check your accuracy. Transfer the curve to the plane. It is best to transfer the lines all the way around the plane (see Figures 9-13 and 9-14).

If the maximum amount of material you have to remove is less than ⅛" (3mm) or so, you can use another plane to shape the bottom, working cross-wise to the length. Otherwise, band saw the waste away and fair the curve with another plane. As the planning approaches the line, back the blade off to make lighter and lighter cuts. If the surface is particularly rough after this, you can smooth it some with a file. It does not have to be very smooth at this point. Check that the area of the sole in front of the mouth is dead straight across, as are the areas at the very head and toe, and that the sole is not twisted (Figures 9-15 and 9-16).

Now here is the crucial part: the sole of the plane must contact the work only at the very front of the plane and at a small area right in front of the mouth. If other areas of the sole contact the work, the plane will ride up and you will have trouble getting a consistent cut. All the other areas of the sole must be relieved so that they do not contact the curve. The amount of relief will determine the accuracy of the curve, especially at the beginning and end of the cut, so you do not want to remove too much: just a few thousandths of an inch.

Figure 9-12.

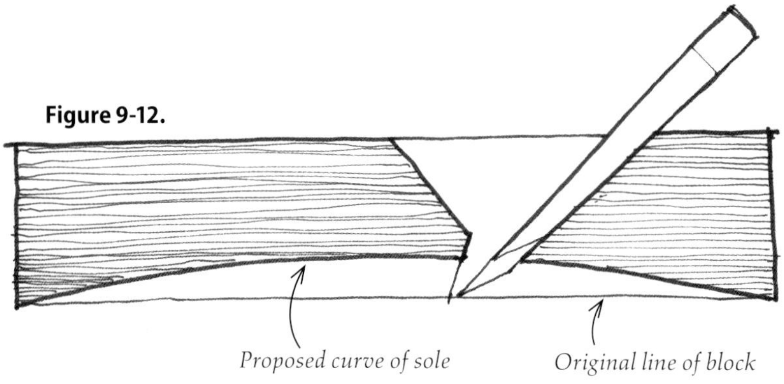

Proposed curve of sole   *Original line of block*

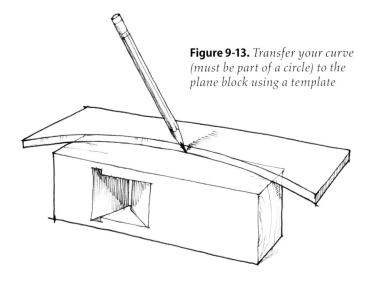

Figure 9-13. *Transfer your curve (must be part of a circle) to the plane block using a template*

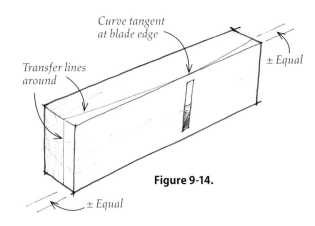

Curve tangent at blade edge

Transfer lines around

± *Equal*

Figure 9-14.

± *Equal*

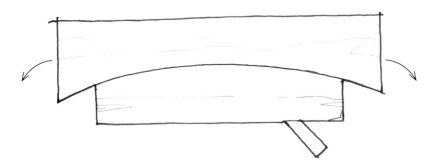

Figure 9-15. *Use the template held against the bottom to check the curve of the sole. Move the template along its length back and forth to compensate for irregularities in the template.*

As well, make sure the area in front of the mouth follows the curve; the closer this area is in matching the curve, the finer you'll be able to set the blade (Figure 9-17). I usually use a card scraper to form these areas, perhaps assisted by some draw-filing to even things up. Give the sole a few degrees of chamfer along its length on either side of the blade; this will reduce the chance these areas will contact the work and interfere with the cut (Figure 9-18).

For convex curves, I have been using a small Japanese-style smoother with a stop screwed to the front. How deep this stop is set determines the radius of the work. This works well except when coming off the curve,

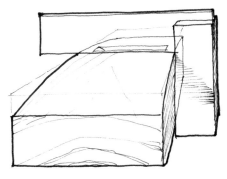

Figure 9-16. *Check along its length with the template and across its width with a square for twist, flatness across its width, and squareness to the sides.*

Figure 9-17.

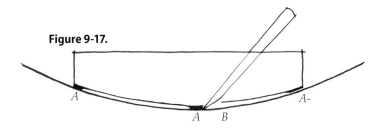

A   A   B   A-

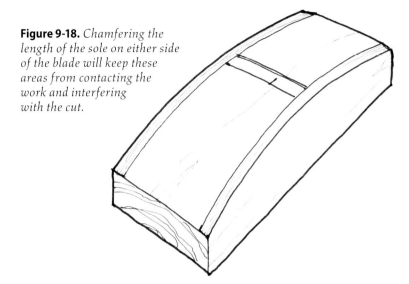

Figure 9-18. *Chamfering the length of the sole on either side of the blade will keep these areas from contacting the work and interfering with the cut.*

Figure 9-19. *Small Japanese planes can be useful in rough-shaping pieces, as the body can be modified to accommodate the shape being sought. I added an adjustable nosepiece to the plane at left to aid in shaping convex curves.*

Figure 9-20.

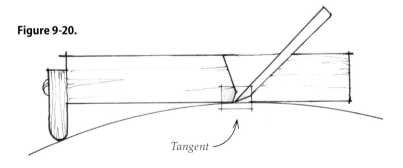

Tangent

as the stop drops off losing the reference point. I have been able to work around this, but technically, you should also put a stop at the back of the plane to help stabilize the plane as the front stop comes off.

Round the bottom of the stop (Figure 9-19). It can be screwed to the plane with machine screws (finer adjustment, greater holding power than a wood screw). Drill the holes in the plane with a drill bit sized to the shank of the screw, and let the screw tap its own threads as you drive it in.

To set the stop, position the plane on the curve of the work and adjust the stop until the blade just contacts the work. Check to see that the stop is parallel to the sole and then tighten the screws. If you also have a stop on the back of the plane, set it also to just contact the surface (Figures 9-20 and 9-21).

Hollowing, Rounding, and Spoonbottom Planes

If you need a hollowing or rounding plane of a specific size or curvature and are modifying a plane, pay particular attention to the geometry of the mouth and throat opening. If you start with a plane with a straight blade, regrind the blade, and re-form the bottom of the plane, the mouth opening, and the chipwell, as well, will no longer be parallel to the edge (Figure 9-22). This is because the throat angle is not parallel to the bed angle and so will open up the more the sole is curved. This may not be a problem if the sole is only slightly curved, or if a fine mouth is not important. However, if the mouth opening is excessive for your needs, you will have to fit a sole plate or *kuchi-ire* to close the mouth down. If you are making a plane from scratch, you must curve the mouth opening and the chipwell to match.

While traditional Western hollow and round planes in the molding-plane style often have a casual mouth opening, formed by the angle of the chipwell that results in a mouth that does not exactly follow the curve of the blade; many times on a bench plane, you may want a tight mouth on a plane with a curved blade in order to reduce tearout. When making such a plane you have two ways to achieve this. The first is to graphically project the curve and cut it directly. The second is to cut the mouth opening and throat at the blade bed angle, not the final throat angle of 70° to 90°, shape the sole, and then cut the throat-relief angle of 70° to 90° to the resulting curve.

To make a spoonbottom plane, which is a compass plane with a convex curved blade, begin with the curve across the width of the plane. Cut the blade bed and mouth opening as described in "Laying Out a Block for Hollowing and Rounding Planes" (page 138). Then, form the curve across the plane's width, and grind and hone the blade to match. Last, form the curve along the length of the plane as described above. Make a template for both curves before you start, and use it to check the work as it progresses.

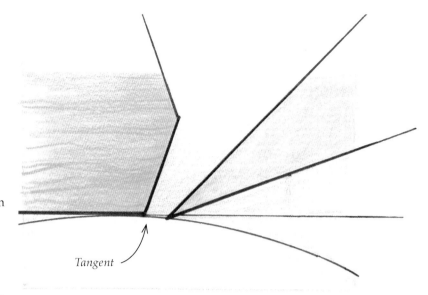

Tangent

Figure 9-21.

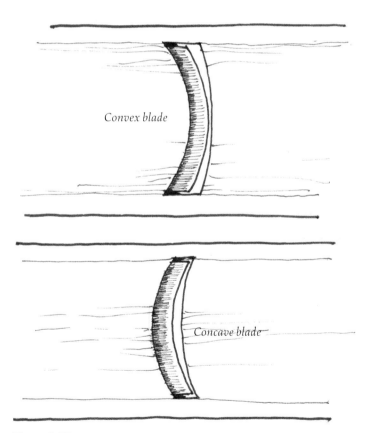

Convex blade

Concave blade

Figure 9-22.

LAYING OUT A BLOCK FOR HOLLOWING AND ROUNDING PLANES

There are two methods for laying out and cutting a block for curved-edge planes: the Graphic Projection Method and the Direct Cutting Method.

GRAPHIC PROJECTION METHOD

Convex-Blade (Hollowing) Plane

Laying Out the Mouth Opening

Laying Out the Mouth Opening

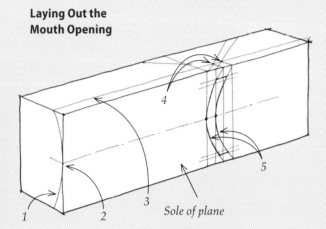

Sole of plane

1   Mark the curve of sole on both ends of the block.

2   Mark the apex of the curve; for a symmetrical curve, this will be the centerline of the block

3   Mark the curve height line down both sides of the block. (If the curve is not symmetric, these may not be the same height.)

4   At the intersection of the curve height line and blade lines draw lines down the side and across the sole at 90° to intersect with the blade width lines and the apex line of the curve.

5   Sketch a curve from the intersection of these lines with the sides of the block to their intersection of the apex line with the mouth line. This is the line of the mouth opening. (If the curve is not symmetrical, it may be helpful to project a few more points to establish the curve.)

Laying Out the Chipwell

Laying Out the Chipwell

blade edge line

Top of plane

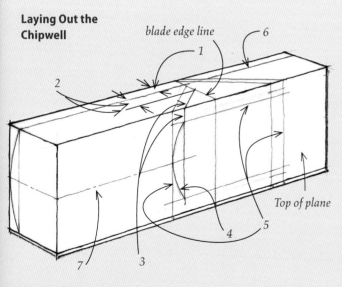

1   Measure the height of the curve.

2   Mark this throat-height dimension up from the intersection of the curve-height line marked on the side with the blade-edge line.

3   Transfer this point to the top of the block at the same angle as the chipwell, and across the top to intersect with the apex line.

4   Sketch a curve from the intersection of this line with the layout line of the side of the chipwell to the intersection of the apex line with the front of the chipwell.

5   Original chipwell layout lines

6   Curve height line

7   Apex of curve

Concave-Blade (Rounding) Plane

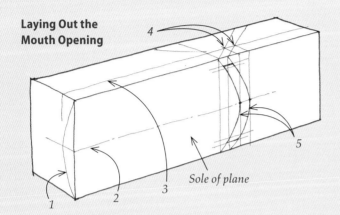

Laying Out the Mouth Opening

Sole of plane

Laying Out the Mouth Opening

1 Mark the curve of sole on both ends of the block.

2 Mark the apex of the curve; for a symmetrical curve this will be the centerline of the block

3 Mark the curve height line down both sides of the block. (If the curve is not symmetric, these may not be the same height.)

4 At the intersection of the curve height line and blade lines, draw lines down the side and across the sole to intersect with the line of the apex of the curve

5 Sketch a curve from the blade lines at either edge of the sole to the intersection of the apex line with the mouth line. This is the line of the mouth opening. (If the curve is not symmetrical, it may be helpful to project a few more points to establish the curve.)

If you cut the chipwell flat and not to a curve similar to the mouth opening, you may end up with very little support at the mouth, or even the chipwell cutting into the final mouth opening. Layout this curve before cutting to make sure you have enough material at the throat.

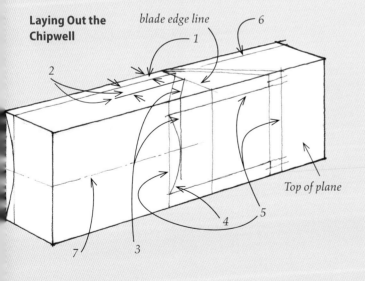

Laying Out the Chipwell

blade edge line

Top of plane

Laying Out the Chipwell

1 Measure the height of the curve.

2 Transfer this dimension up from the curve height line to the blade edge line.

3 Transfer this point to the top of the block at the same angle as the chipwell, and across the top to intersect with the apex line.

4 Sketch a curve from the intersection of this line with the apex line to the corners of the original chipwell layout

5 Original chipwell layout lines

6 Curve height line

7 Apex of curve

CUTTING A BLOCK FOR HOLLOWING AND ROUNDING PLANES

GRAPHIC PROJECTION METHOD *(continued)*

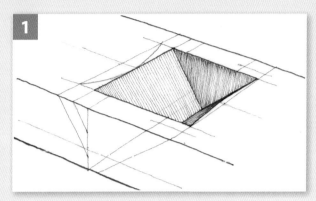

1 Cut open the opening for the blade as you would for a regular plane, chiseling to the high point of the curve of the chipwell.

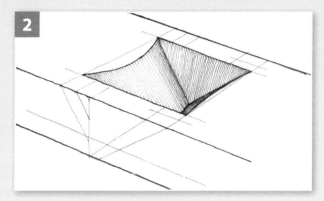

2 Form the curve of the chipwell.

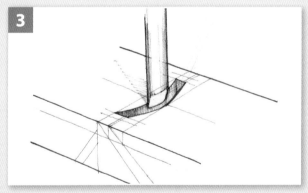

3 Turn the block over and begin cutting the mouth opening. Chisel straight down—90° to the sole—on the line of the mouth, making a relief cut to free the chip back from the blade-bed line. Continue until you break through. Finish forming the blade bed.

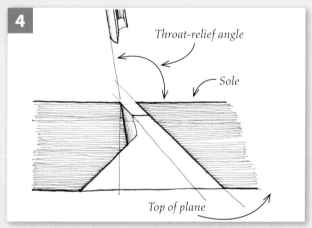

4 Pare the mouth open as required. Increase the throat-relief angle if you can.

DIRECT CUTTING METHOD

If your blade edge curve is a section of a circle, the **Graphic Projection Method** (page 138) produces reasonable results. Curves that are more complex could also be projected in such a manner, but it is not practical to project very many points accurately on such a small scale. For this reason, and the fact that I often make mistakes in projecting my points, I most often use this method for cutting the mouth opening.

With this method, you need to verify that you have enough wood left at the throat after cutting the curve of the mouth, so you may still need to graphically project the curve of the wall of the chipwell. This is especially true with a concave sole (rounding) plane. Refer to pages 138 and 139 for laying out and cutting the chipwell.

If you cut the chipwell flat and not to a curve similar to the mouth opening, you may end up with very little support at the mouth, or even with the chipwell cutting into the final mouth opening. Layout this curve before cutting to make sure you have enough material at the throat.

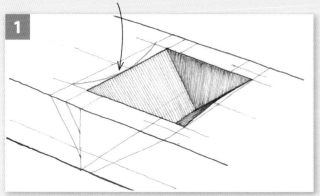

1 Cut open the opening for the blade as you would for a regular plane, chiseling to the high point of the curve of the chipwell.

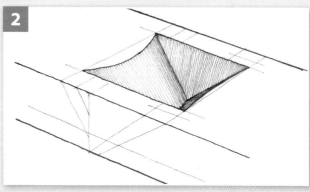

2 Form the curve of the chipwell.

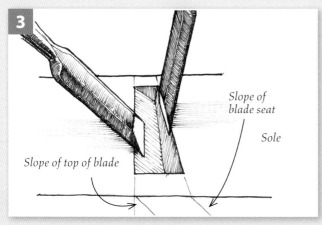

3 After the chipwell and blade seat are fully excavated, make a V-cut to open the mouth on the bottom. The slope of the front cut at the mouth should match that of the top of the blade. The back cut at the blade seat is more vertical.

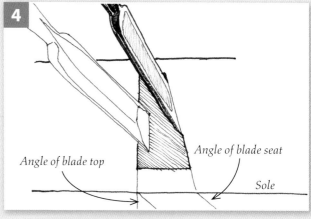

4 Continue cutting the mouth opening on the bottom with the front cut at the angle of the top of the blade, but the back cut (at the blade seat) increasingly undercut toward the angle of the blade seat.

LAYING OUT AND CUTTING THE MOUTH OPENING FOR HOLLOWING AND ROUNDING PLANES (CONTINUED)

DIRECT CUTTING METHOD *(continued)*

5

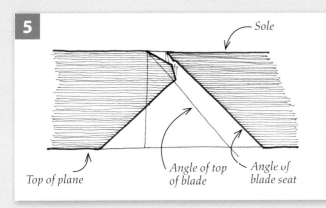

Sole

Top of plane

Angle of top of blade

Angle of blade seat

5   Alternate chiseling down from the top of the plane at the angle of the blade seat and from the sole, deepening the cut while opening it to the angles of the blade top and seat. Eventually you will break through.

6

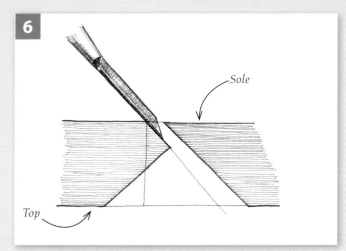

Sole

Top

6   Finish paring the opening down from both the top and bottom until you have a clean slot at the mouth parallel at the front to the angle of the blade top and at the back to the blade-seat angle.

7

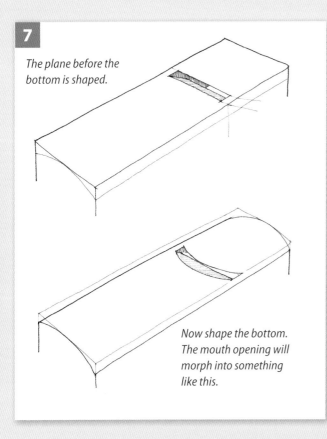

The plane before the bottom is shaped.

Now shape the bottom. The mouth opening will morph into something like this.

8

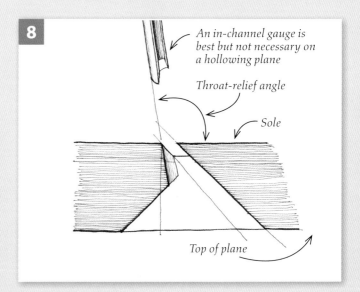

An in-channel gauge is best but not necessary on a hollowing plane

Throat-relief angle

Sole

Top of plane

7   Shape the bottom.

8   Pare the throat-relief angle back to the curve of the mouth opening.

INDEX